The Revd Dr Ali Green first trained and
becoming co-founder and director of an
has spent many years in ministry in par.
as a lay leader, Reader, deacon and, latterly, as a priest. She worked
for several years as a chaplain and lecturer in a male prison, and is
currently a priest in the diocese of Monmouth. Her PhD in theology
was awarded by Roehampton University. She is the Wales representative for the Ecumenical Forum of European Christian Women. She
has been married for thirty years and is a mother and grandmother.

A THEOLOGY OF WOMEN'S PRIESTHOOD

ALI GREEN

First published in Great Britain in 2009

Society for Promoting Christian Knowledge
36 Causton Street
London SW1P 4ST

British Library Cataloguing-in-Publication Data
A catalogue record for this book is available from the British Library

ISBN 978–0–281–06089–4

1 3 5 7 9 10 8 6 4 2

Typeset by Graphicraft Limited, Hong Kong
Printed in Great Britain by Ashford Colour Press

Produced on paper from sustainable forests

Contents

v

Acknowledgements

I am most grateful to Professor Tina Beattie who has offered me so much support and encouragement in my research and preparation for this book. Thanks also to the many friends and colleagues who talked to me, offered suggestions and shared their personal experiences and insights. My task was greatly helped by the wonderful staff of Sarum Library who never failed to find me every book and document I asked for. And finally thanks to Dave, who supported me with affection, good humour and hot meals while I was labouring at the type face.

1

Introduction – a collision of symbolic meanings?

We usually need time to reflect on significant events and changes in our lives, and then to apply that reflection to the way that we see and act in the world. This is often the way we do theology. We respond in faith to what happens, and then on reflection we develop and refine our theology accordingly.

Bishop Gene Robinson, who is in an openly gay relationship, recently recounted a conversation he had about his controversial election and consecration with Archbishop Rowan Williams. According to Robinson, the Archbishop felt that the theological and pastoral issues should have been hammered out before Robinson took the final step toward episcopacy. The bishop replied that 'all the great steps towards justice the church has taken have been the result of our somehow finding the courage to do the right thing and then thinking it through later – not the other way around' (2008:123).

Bishop Gene's remarks about the Church's debate on homosexuality could equally well apply to that around the issue of women's priesthood – and indeed to the historical place of women in the Church. Women have always got on with following God's call, and theology and church practice have eventually caught up with them. I mention a few such women in the following pages. Mary Magdalene, Apostle to the Apostles, pioneered a witnessing role for women that is only now being fully realized. Mary Wollstonecraft argued for girls to be educated and for women to become full members of society at a time when females were generally thought unfit for learning or leadership. Maude Royden courageously exercised her gift of preaching years before the Anglican Church accepted women in the pulpit. The first women ordinands defended and pursued their call to vocation in the absence of a thoroughgoing theology that took account of their distinctness as women. Now that substantial numbers of women are exercising their priestly ministry in the

Anglican Church, an examination of the theology of women's priesthood is timely.

In this book I develop a theology that treats sexual difference as a basic philosophical category. To treat sexual difference seriously requires a fundamental shift in our religious thinking, which itself influences our cultural environment. It runs counter to traditional ways of thinking and acting that leave women without a voice. It asserts that there is another way of being that is equally capable of mediating divine presence. It exposes the hiatus between women's lives and their religion which has always existed within a male-dominated social, ecclesiastical and academic hierarchy, and shows how the woman priest can bridge that gap.

The traditional all-male priesthood is embedded in its own masculine ways of knowing, of language and of behaviour. It carries with it an array of symbolic meanings and associations that influence the way the Church regards women and the way women in the Church see themselves. The relationship between the Church and women has never been straightforward, and the root of the difficulties lies in sexual difference. I once met a fellow priest who had striking auburn hair which, although very short, reminded me of the figures who appear in many Pre-Raphaelite paintings. When I mentioned this to her, she remarked rather wistfully that in the past her hair had reached down almost to her waist. But she had cut it off when she was testing her vocation because someone had advised her that she would never be accepted for ordination while she had long, flaming locks. What was it, I wondered, about her hair that the church authorities (then almost exclusively male) found so problematic? Were they anxious because it was too strong a signifier of female sexuality? There are lots of symbolic associations around sexuality and women, as there are around the priesthood; and those who were selecting future ordinands seemed to find in my colleague an irreconcilable collision in these associations.

Symbols, as the philosopher Paul Ricoeur has shown, give rise to thought. They illumine and give order to human experience, and so help us to find and understand human reality. For example, when we hear the word 'stain', we might think of a dirty mark or a blot. But we might also go on to think of moral connotations such as defilement and depravity. The symbol points to something beyond itself that allows us to reflect on complex, abstract concepts. Barack

Obama's victory in the 2008 American elections was widely acknowledged as much more than electoral success for a particular candidate or party. It was hailed as a symbol of hope and justice for millions of African Americans and other minority groups in a country still tainted with racism.

Because it carries virtually inexhaustible meanings, a symbol can point towards the world of the sacred. So we use words such as 'life' or 'blood' not only to define physical things and events but to denote abstract spiritual ideas that cannot be confined to precise definitions. The symbol is subject to a great range of linguistic and cultural diversity, so it always has to be interpreted; and there is always more than one interpretation. So symbol and the process of interpretation work hand in hand since, as Ricoeur says, 'We must understand in order to believe, but we must believe in order to understand' (1967:351).

Where some event occurs that changes the identity of the priesthood, then there is change also to the symbolism and narrative shared by the community of faith. Three symbols associated with priesthood are those of the body, the bride and the whore; and these are all especially resonant now that priests in the Anglican Church include women. My aim in this book is to begin to develop a theology of women's priesthood by looking at the symbol and narrative of Christian religion, including the metaphors of the body, the bride and the whore which each form a recurring theme through its scripture and tradition.

Body matters

God-talk these days, it seems, is littered with bodies. Current Christian theology, concerned as it is with themes of identity and relationship, characteristically starts from the perspective of the embodied nature of people as members of the Body of Christ. It considers individual and communal experience of the numinous: the immanence, the now-ness of God embodied in the universe, in humanity and in the community of faith. This notion of embodiment is expressed in the Eucharist, the central act of Anglican worship, in which, through the action of the Holy Spirit, Christ is made present to worshippers, and through which the life and identity of the Church is affirmed and renewed. From my own confessional

3

standpoint as an Anglican, I understand the Eucharist as central to God's continuing self-revelation. It is a sacramental re-enactment of a historical event, a ceremonial banquet and a sacrifice shared by the whole community which forms the nexus between the narrative of faith and the praxis of discipleship.

The symbols of faith do not stand alone but derive meaning from the Christian narrative. In celebrating the Eucharist, as in other ritual acts, the body cannot be ignored. Indeed, the eucharistic liturgy, including those actions performed by the priest, can be understood as a bodily narrative whereby God's presence is affirmed in and through the material fabric of human existence (for an exploration of this see Power, 1984). Through the narrative of the text – that is, through both telling and enacting the faith story – the liturgy gives shape to the identity and experience of the individual and of the community, and points towards what is to come. The words and actions of the priest at the altar retell and re-enact the story of faith in order that worshippers are affirmed and strengthened, and make a response. We are reminded of our part in the grand narrative, our inheritance from the past and our future destiny, within the continuing Christian story. The narrative of priest and congregation is embedded in an ancient history continually re-membered in the form of symbol and story, and therefore open through successive generations to fresh interpretation and insight. Hence worship requires a reciprocal commitment and action. Our response to God in our daily actions is focused – indeed initiated – in the ritual action of the liturgy, and in particular of the Eucharist, the focus of worship and of discipleship.

The eucharistic ritual is pregnant with transformative possibilities, using natural symbols rooted in daily life that point toward the divine in order to form and mould discipleship and ministry. Through the liturgy, we continuously reinterpret ultimate realities that cannot be expressed through intellectual effort alone. Liturgy holds the tension between ordinary experience and the numinous. Part of that liturgy involves the recitation of the Eucharistic Prayer, spoken by the priest, who represents Christ to the Church and to the whole community, and represents them before God. The priest here has a key symbolic function, becoming part of the language of symbolic communication. The priest's cultic actions are drawn from common life but point beyond it, articulating in word and action the relationship between society and its sacred things.

The priest, as celebrant, shares and reflects the faith of the community present, and also of the Church worldwide and the Church throughout history. In taking bread, breaking and consecrating it, the priest acts in the name of Christ, of the local congregation and of the Catholic Church down through history. In the Anglican Communion, there has been a recent and significant change. From 1976 in the United States, from 1994 in England and 1997 in Wales, and in many other provinces, celebrants at the altar have included priests who are women. For the first time in the history of the Anglican Church, all members of a congregation have had the opportunity to receive the sacraments both from someone of their own sex and from a member of the opposite sex.

The woman priest at the altar is visibly and audibly a representative of the feminine/female. (By this I mean that she embodies both the biological characteristics and the traits of behaviour and outlook traditionally ascribed to her sex within a cultural context. From now on, to avoid cumbersome language, I will simply use the term feminine to cover this range of meaning and the term 'masculine' when meaning 'masculine/male' i.e., the biological and cultural characteristics ascribed to men.) Hence the woman priest causes a shift in the symbolism associated with priesthood itself, because it is now a priesthood not of one sex but of both sexes. It is a shift that causes us to look again at how we understand and respond to God, how we interpret Scripture, how we worship and how we live as Christians in the world.

Priesthood and sexuality

Does the priest who is a woman really bring such changes – theologically, liturgically and morally – to Christian teaching and life? I would suggest that she does, not least from the evidence of those who oppose the priesting of women. The argument against female clergy rests on an understanding of the symbolic nature of priesthood. On the one hand, the argument is based on the meaning of the priest being *in persona Christi* (in the person of Christ). Since Christ's incarnation was as a man, then only a man can adequately incarnate Christ for the priesthood of the Church. On the other hand, the biblical argument used against women priests rests on the notion of Christ's headship over the Church, which has traditionally been taken to model the relationship between husband and wife, and more broadly between men and women. Paul's constraints on women as leaders were taken as a prescription for all time (see, for instance, 1 Cor. 11.3–16; Eph. 5.22–24).

Thomas Hopko, an Orthodox Christian, has written about changes in worship that have occurred in churches with ordained women (1999:250). He links these with changing expectations and personal behaviour of clergy, and wonders what will happen to churches that allow the ordination of

> women, together with the physically challenged people, the more than once married, the sexually active unmarried, those married to persons who are not members of their churches, those convicted of public crimes, and others who traditionally would have been disqualified from pastoral service in their churches.　　　　(1999:250)

Hopko does not clarify why women should be linked with the other groups he names, nor why such groups should indeed be barred from ordained ministry. But the alarm he expresses illustrates how the figure of the woman priest has broken open a huge range of further meanings and interpretations. This in turn calls for another look at the nature of what is signified – the divine and ourselves in relation to God and to each other.

The long road towards the ordination of women exposed how important gender and sexuality are in the interpretation of priesthood. That women were (and arguably still are) viewed by church authorities largely in terms of their sex and of their relationship to men is revealed in this comment made by the Archbishops' Commission on the priesthood of women in 1936:

> The ministration of women will tend to produce a lowering of the spiritual tone of Christian worship . . . it would be impossible for the male members to be present at a service at which a woman ministered without becoming unduly conscious of her sex.
> 　　　　　　　　　　　　　　　　　　　　(Furlong, 1991:41)

Tales abound of abhorrence at the idea of pregnant, long-haired and/or attractive women presiding at the altar. There is apparently an anxiety (evident in those advising my auburn-haired colleague) that women's bodiliness and sexuality present a distraction from the spiritual. And this preoccupation itself exposes the problem that the Church has always had in the matter of the relationship between women and men. Una Kroll, preaching in January 2007 at a Eucharist to mark the tenth anniversary of the ordination of the first women priests (including herself) in Wales, commented:

> We are seeing on our TV screens, in news reels, at public events like baptisms, weddings and funerals ordinary sinful women and men working alongside each other, contributing their ordinary gifts, making mistakes, bringing forth old and new treasures in heaven, ambassadors of Christ.

At a celebratory service, these were words of affirmation and of hope. Yet this vision of a fruitful partnership between the sexes has not always been the experience of clergywomen in the Province of Wales or elsewhere. During a conference at St Michael's Theological College, Cardiff, to reflect on the decade of women priests in Wales, I heard numerous accounts from dedicated female clergy of the problems they have faced in collaborating with male colleagues who themselves had difficulties in having to work alongside women. Joanna Penberthy, reporting on a previous conference where the issue of men and women clergy working together was raised, writes:

> Women who have come from other fields of employment and are used to working alongside men can find the way they are treated within the church rather a rude awakening. The fact that as we discussed these problems, the women in the room could not begin to imagine how our male colleagues might react to the suggestion of gender equality awareness training points perhaps to the scale of the problem that the Church in Wales faces in normalizing the role of women within the ordained ministry. (Bayley, 2006:16)

Among delegates at the conference in Cardiff were some who had been among the first cohort of women ordained as priests in Wales in 1997. There was clearly a still lingering sense of pain and hurt, and a felt need for continued affirmation and support. No doubt such feelings exist also among some male clergy and laypeople, both women and men. Robin Greenwood, in the year in which the first women were priested in England, stated:

we should be foolish not to expect acute anxiety and stress arising from the renewed understanding of women's authority in a church where men have for so long assumed the right to govern alone and where women have been largely defined as helpers and supporters.

(1994:43)

Those who pioneered the way have carried an enormous weight of responsibility, including that of addressing the anxiety and stress caused by the priesting of women, and the reluctance, hesitancy or even outright opposition of some male clergy and laypeople. Those women who now follow their pioneering colleagues have benefited from that struggle as women's priesthood becomes more accepted. The enriched symbolic possibilities attached to the woman priest bring with them an imperative for action and change. Female clergy need to be conscious of their own potent symbolic charge if they are to promote a transformation in the religious mind that brings to birth women's full selfhood and a redemptive, liberating partnership between the sexes.

Women who are aware of these transformative possibilities are more likely to be able to take steps in their ministry to make such possibilities a reality. Clergy who are conscious of the symbolic significance of both sexual difference in general and the (as yet largely unexplored) feminine in particular can potentially harness that awareness in renewing and revitalizing the symbolism attached to the divine, to the priesthood and to the Church's understanding of itself as the Body of Christ. Yet how aware are current ordinands of their predecessors' ground-breaking efforts, even over the last twenty or so years, let alone as far back as Maude Royden and the like? Jean Cornell, in an article on women priests and the episcopate, comments that 'women clergy are surprisingly ignorant of the debt owed to Christian feminists and their role in the promotion of women's ordination; this needs to be remedied' (2003:43).

Those who have only recently become priests may well not be fully versed in the history and theology around the issue of women's ordination. And yet this later generation is the one which, having reserves of energy and youth not exhausted by the original struggle, must carry forward the vision for full recognition and selfhood not only for women priests but for women everywhere. It would be helpful for all ordinands, as part of their ministerial training, to learn of the history and circumstances that have led to the eventual ordination of women, and to study the theology around the issue of women's priesthood. When we acknowledge sexual difference then we understand that the advent of the woman's voice in the sacred space initiates not an adjustment to the status quo but the promise (or threat) of radical, irreversible transformation. The responsibility of bringing to speech that silenced voice rests at least in part with the woman priest, who opens up the symbolism around priesthood and the Eucharist, God and the Body of Christ. In this way she is on the cutting edge of a new understanding and experience of being Church.

An analogical approach

Garrison Keillor, recalling his Protestant childhood in *Lake Wobegon Days*, recounts how his Brethren family worshipped: no priest, no pictures, no musical instruments, but a lot of extemporary prayer, Bible study and quoting of Scripture. He confesses his secret curiosity about the goings-on in the local Roman Catholic church, with its feast days, blessings of animals, glamorous processions and ocarina band. The young Garrison suspected that while his family were worshipping quietly in a bare living-room, 'not far away the Catholics were whooping it up' (1986:103).

Keillor vividly illustrates the varying degree to which symbolism is overtly expressed in the liturgy. In the Anglo-Catholic tradition, a rich symbolism is conveyed by the priest, by various objects and by choreographed gesture and movement. The cycle of seasons, feast days and religious drama is strictly observed. Ritual may include processions, the lighting of candles, the wearing of particular garments and colours, the use of incense and bells and the adoption of certain gestures by the priest, particularly during the Eucharistic Prayer. This analogical expression characterizes the approach of the Catholic tradition and of the predominant language of Catholic theology. Protestant traditions tend in varying degrees to have much less elaborate ritual and dramatic presentation. The emphasis is rather on the dialectical – teaching and hearing the Word through the reading and interpretation of Scripture, appealing more to the intellect than to a deep, perhaps unconscious, response to symbol. Word is paramount in expressing the holy, and discourse takes primacy over the power of holy things and actions to reveal the numinous.

I am speaking here more from an Anglo-Catholic than from a low Evangelical position. Of course we experience the presence of God in our daily routine and through intellectual discourse, but for me it is also through rituals, symbols and myths that I find I am able to approach the reality of the sacred. Hence the value of reflecting on the narrative and symbol within the Eucharistic Prayer as it is recited by the priest, since it is at this moment, of all ritual events in the Christian liturgy, that the present has the potential to become most saturated with the power of the sacred.

When the Eucharistic Prayer is spoken by a woman priest, there is a shift, a fluidity, perhaps even a shock, in the symbolic charge. The presence of a woman celebrant in the Anglican Church is relatively new, so that the symbolic associated with her remains as yet novel, unstable and evolving. Moreover, her presence invites further reflection on the symbolic nature of the priesthood as a whole, since it brings up the question of genderization of symbol and of narrative, and therefore of what (in a historically all-male priesthood) has previously been overlooked or excluded from the normative. The narrative of the liturgy, and the hearing of it by the congregation of worshippers, inform and shape the sense of identity of the individual and of the community. Yet this narrative has largely omitted a vast area of human experience, because it has mostly reflected the masculine and has overlooked the feminine. Since the Christian narrative is signified and retold by the priest, the question arises as to whether a hitherto exclusively male priesthood was ever able sufficiently to reveal the nature of the divine or to represent the whole Church. The male priest, inheriting such a long history of male-only priesthood within a highly patriarchal institution, is unavoidably associated with the traditions and attitudes of that institution and the culture in which it is embedded.

The symbols associated with the texts of priest and liturgy are overwhelmingly weighted with androcentric meanings and referents, and tend to be interpreted from a male perspective. They have become ossified by this gendered exclusivity, and so, being restrictive rather than liberating, are no longer able to express an adequate correlation with final revelation. Women have historically made a place for themselves within an unequally gendered narrative and liturgy. But the biased way in which the faith story has been retold and re-enacted has helped neither women nor men to reach a mature sense of identity as equal creatures of God within the community of faith.

Bride and whore

The Christian story has been retold and refigured by a range of faith communities according to their own circumstances and aspirations, often offering interpretations that have changed over time. Among the great themes of the Christian narrative are those of the bride and groom, the husband and wife. These reflect the patriarchal interpretations and assumptions about the relationship between women, men and God current not only at the early development of the stories but also through the history of their refiguration as they have been interpreted through the ages.

We can detect a gendered perspective in many recurring images in both Hebrew and Christian Scripture, including the marital one. Associated with the notion of covenant, Yahweh is depicted as the husband of Israel and, in the New Testament, the Church is the bride. The image occurs, for instance, in the Song of Songs (5.1), interpreted in Jewish rabbinic literature as an expression of God's love for his spouse, Israel. In Isaiah, God is described as both the maker and husband of Zion (54.5), and he rejoices over Zion as a bridegroom over his bride (62.5). Jerusalem, representing the people of God, is described variously as a forsaken wife, a barren woman, a daughter and a woman in labour. With the birth of the Church, this female figure of Hebrew Scripture came to embody all those whom Christ has redeemed. Jesus alludes to the traditional image of God as husband and Israel as unfaithful wife when he talks of 'this adulterous and sinful generation' (Mark 8.38). Paul takes up the nuptial theme when he refers to members of the Church as children of God's promise, whose mother is Jerusalem, the heavenly city of God (Gal. 4.21–31). The author of Revelation uses the imagery of a wedding to express the intimate relationship between Christ and the Church, for instance when an angel commands the writer to record 'Blessed are those who are invited to the marriage supper of the Lamb!' (Rev. 19.9). The new Jerusalem, the heavenly city, is likened to a bride 'beautifully adorned for her husband' (21.2). Another image is that of the adulterous wife, which was often adopted to depict the unfaithfulness of God's chosen people. For instance,

God warns Moses that, after he has died, the people will 'prostitute themselves to the foreign gods of the land into which they are going' (Deut. 31.16); and Judges records how Israel prostituted itself by worshipping Gideon's ephod (Judg. 8.27). The God-as-husband image, then, says something of the perfect relationship between God and people that is the divine intent, and also of the broken relationship pertaining in the fallen world. The metaphorical bride or wife of Scripture is not only in a position of inequality and submission, correlating to the status of women in the period that the text was written; she has also often been redeemed from a state of whoredom.

The problem for us today is that, in society that upholds the principle of sexual equality, many of the ancient, traditional symbols associated with women have become unfamiliar, inappropriate or even downright offensive. Indeed, some texts have been criticized as ignoring or denying women's experience, dignity and subjectivity (for more on this, see Chapter 2). With this in mind, I want to look for a symbolic space for the feminine that is distinct and appropriate for real women. Key to my argument here is the concept of sexual difference within the narrative of faith. Women are commonly defined by their gender and sexuality, and feminine bodily metaphors are usually predicated on the masculine imaginary (that is, the images and dynamics on which thoughts are based). To put it simply, we live in a man's world where women's sense of identity has always been largely defined by men.

The male-dominated church has historically assumed that women's biological functions make them more vulnerable to sin, more dangerous and more needful of control since they are closer to the earth and to the influences of nature. Many older women in the Anglican Church remember when women could neither preach, read the lesson nor enter the chancel; they made a vow of obedience at their wedding, remember a male-only Readership and possibly are scandalized by the idea of female priesthood. Yet many modern women, used to inclusive language and equal status (at least ostensibly) at home and in their workplace, are discouraged in their faith by attending a church led by an authoritarian male priest, where the hymns use male-dominated language and are led by an all-male choir, where they are taught from the pulpit to submit to male authority and where women's roles are restricted largely to the pews. Such women often find this tradition off-putting and denying of women's gifts, experience and value. Indeed, some women have repudiated the Church altogether as irredeemably discriminatory.

I want to move beyond the traditional, dualistic interpretation of physiological, intellectual or spiritual superiority or inferiority, and to explore the distinctiveness in the identity of the feminine. And I want to make the case that this distinctiveness in sexual difference should be acknowledged, explored, celebrated and included fully within the liturgy and the life of the Church. The concept of sexual difference has a meaningful bearing on the woman priest and her interaction with worshippers' perception, experience and understanding of their identity and vocation as members of the Body of Christ. Taking the woman priest as the locus of interpretation, we can explore symbols and narratives of our faith story to demonstrate the value of the feminine, which in turn invites a response that liberates us from traditional masculine and patriarchal ways of hearing, understanding and responding to our faith story.

What women's priesthood stands for must not make it harder for women to belong to the Church which is part of a world that devalues female experience. Rather, women should be able to see the Church as a community of liberation and of reconciliation. The woman priest has a part to play in overturning old symbols that are outdated and in reinvigorating others so as to offer new meanings. She does this by challenging inculturated assumptions and inviting new insights into the nature of the divine, of the priesthood and of the Church. She also causes us to re-evaluate our gendered response to the Christian narrative. Women's narratives are different from men's narratives; women's interpretation of and response to narratives are different from those of men. The female priest exposes gendered aspects of the story of faith that have hitherto remained unrecognized by masculine interpretations, and invokes a response that opens up questions of gendered difference.

In this sense, the woman priest serves to retrieve or re-member those narratives which may be helpful in informing women, whatever their cultural or social background, of their true identity as children of God. Moreover, she helps us to hear again those Christian narratives which have traditionally been interpreted through a masculine lens, often to the detriment of the identity and status of all women. In short, in retrieving the value and integrity of the feminine, she can be instrumental in achieving a greater sense of self for women in a culture that has historically been informed and dominated by a male religious imagination. She is one part of that subtly shifting narrative which lends the Church a meaningful identity to a wider community where, at least in the West, there has been significant advancement in the economic, political and social status of women.

A new symbolic order

Yet, we might ask, can a Christian woman ever know her true identity and realize her full personhood when the entire symbolic and narrative of her faith has been constructed, ordered and interpreted by men and focused on a masculine divinity? Indeed, can any man similarly reach his horizon of potential within a tradition where sexual difference has been ignored? To explore this issue I am making use of the work of the French feminist thinker Luce Irigaray. She sees the recognition and opening up of sexual difference as a major philosophical project and the paradigm for all other differences, including those in spiritual experience: 'Sexual difference is probably the issue in our time which could be our "salvation" if we thought it through' (1993:5). Her project is to imagine a future grounded in sexual difference, a world beyond patriarchy founded on the acknowledgement of and respect for two equal genders. Her work, largely concerned with symbol and language, looks at failures within the present symbolic order and posits possibilities for fundamental changes built upon sexual difference and recognition of the female subject.

Her quest is for a re-articulation of the present order so as to achieve conditions that would allow women to become subjects in their own right. In this she is trying to imagine the unimaginable, since we have no experience of a possible alternative to our current masculine way of thinking and discourse. Women's identity and means of expression still have to be created. Yet Irigaray insists that, even in present Western culture, where identity, logic and rationality are symbolically male, it is possible to transform the way we imagine and think so that woman can become a subject of culture. It would require a collective transformation of the symbolic built upon recognition of sexual difference: this is, for Irigaray, 'one of the great hopes for the future' (1993:vi).

Irigaray observes that we need divinity in order to become free, autonomous and sovereign; and yet Christianity has been dominated by a male God, created in men's image, with no reference to the female. The female divine is absent. So woman has no selfhood, no divine horizon of her own by which she can become the whole person she is created to be. Irigaray's response to this problem is to call for a rebirth for women, which can take place only when woman is freed from man's archaic projection on to her, and with the advent of an autonomous and positive representation of women's sexuality in culture (1993:17). Woman must be able to become divine in and of herself, not just as mother/lover/wife, in order for a notion of divinity for women to develop. Moreover, we need to find a language that recognizes women's own bodily experience and the range of symbols around the maternal body so that all women can discover their distinctive sexual identity (1993:19). What might be the implications, Irigaray asks, of supposing that women are subjects who can mediate the divine, that the divine can be approached and apprehended through the feminine as well as through the masculine? Such a question opens up a whole range of possibilities for investigating and reinterpreting the array of traditional Christian symbols and narratives, particularly in relation to the woman priest. The fact of women's priesthood in the Anglican Church indicates an acceptance that women can indeed mediate the divine; yet so much of traditional symbol and narrative, in both text and ritual, implicitly or explicitly denies, represses or ignores such a female mediation. Looking at symbols and meanings attached to priesthood reveals ways in which the female priest can indeed represent the female mediation of the divine. This can be achieved, I believe, not through rejecting our story of faith and our ritual expression of it, but through reinterpreting these through a feminist lens which notices what is missing and reads between the lines of traditional ways of thought and interpretation. When we acknowledge gender as a fundamental constituent of identity, then priesthood itself, in its symbolic role of representing the divine, must recognize, value and celebrate its doubly gendered nature as well as that of the whole Body of Christ.

The woman priest breaks the male monopoly on representing the divine, and so opens up possibilities for a female symbolic and for women as subjects of culture. She represents the ability of women everywhere to mediate the divine, not by escaping from but by celebrating their embodied, gendered nature. From this flows the promise of flourishing to all women – and to men also, through the destabilization of the traditional symbolic of godlikeness, power and domination associated with the masculine. Where difference is recognized, respected and cultivated, women and men together can become equal co-redeemers of the world.

Irigaray's search for a divine that is mediated within and between women as well as men, and that allows both sexes to flourish, is taken up by Grace Jantzen. She understands the divine as entirely immanent, inseparable from the world and the material. She is impatient with a traditional philosophy of religion that argues endlessly about the salvation of immortal souls 'in a world where many of the souls being discussed would find salvation here and now in a bowl of food' (1998:111). Her work focuses on the connection between religion and ethical responsiveness, for instance in the spheres of social justice and environmental stewardship. In *Becoming Divine* (1998) and subsequent works, Jantzen seeks to replace the traditional dualism of spirit/matter, mind/body and to identify the divine with the embodied world. She argues that male-dominated thought has focused on death, with a corresponding interest in other worlds and some form of afterlife. With this comes a lack of focus on the needs of the embodied, material world. She cites evidence from Freud and from the development of psychoanalysis to show the conceptual connection in male-dominated culture between women and death, stemming from a young child's experience of separation from the mother and their entry into a male-dominated society. Death thus becomes associated with women's bodies, while the symbolic that links death, sex and the female silences women and ignores or suppresses the significance of birth. She observes that Western philosophy's concern with violence, sacrifice and death – a male concern evident throughout recorded history – is built upon mortality as a fundamental philosophical category, which leads to a longing to escape the constraints of this world, and particularly the gendered body, in preparation for the next world. There is, in other words, a simultaneous fascination with death and a yearning to escape from it. In seeking a reversal of the masculine preoccupation with death, she concludes that we must take account of ourselves as natals (those who are born) as much as mortals (those who will die). Drawing on the work of Hannah Arendt and Heidegger she asks what would happen if we were to start not with death but instead with birth; that is, if we were to treat natality as a foundational concept, and afford it the same serious-ness as mortality and as striving for another world. The notion of birth rather than death is rooted in the maternal, the body and the material, and so it leads not out of this world but towards this world and other people.

Being concerned with the here-and-now, concrete world means wanting all people, women and men, to flourish. This would include giving a voice to women: 'the possibility of women learning to speak as women is in reciprocal relation to becoming (woman) subjects' (1998:147). Part of the process of bringing women to speech is to search religious and philosophical texts for what has been left out by masculine thought and to find a space for natality. In this way, women will be able to enter into the language of culture and so to become subjects (1998:170). But this cannot be done by discourse alone. Human flourishing requires actions as well as thought, as I shall discuss in the course of this book.

Jantzen, in developing her notion of natality, does not expand on any particular religious symbols. I believe, however, that natality, as well as the idea of a female divine horizon, can help us to investigate the 'collision' – in my view, a liberating and fruitful one – that occurs between women's priesthood and religious symbols and narrative. We can apply these notions to the Eucharist as it is celebrated with and among believers in the Anglican community. The redemptive process involves being divinely guided in righting broken relation-ships, including those of gender, in the concrete world. This should not be simply a case of abstract intellectual discourse but a practical move toward justice in human relationships. Where human relation-ships truly echo the divine, then the voices of all, including those as yet without a voice, will be heard into speech. Moreover, as Irigaray speaks of the redemptive potential of sexual difference, where both male and female identity is allowed to flourish, then a priesthood of two equal genders that recognizes and respects sexual difference is more likely to be a redemptive priesthood that allows and encour-ages all people to achieve their full identity as children of God.

So does the symbol of the woman priest at the altar offer new and recovered meanings in the realm of the transcendent? Does it also serve to initiate social renewal in the invitation to decision and action? Or is the feminine represented in the woman priest simply to be ignored, so that she is regarded as an 'honorary man', whose gender is of no import and who is laden therefore with symbolism identical to that of the male priest? These are some of the questions I want to tackle here.

The following chapters are divided into three paired sets, each beginning with an extract from the Eucharistic Prayer (in this case Prayer A). From this starting point, I summarize first the 'received wisdom' of traditional theologies, and then explore how the priest who is a woman extends worshippers' understanding of themselves as the Body of Christ in relationship with the divine, with each other and with the world. From each phrase taken from the Eucharistic Prayer I explore a variety of themes. Chapters 2 and 3 examine the notion of humans created in the image of God, the lack of women's sense of self and the potential contribution of the female priesthood to enable all people, female and male, to achieve full personhood. Chapters 4 and 5, through the symbolism of bread, look at our relationship with the divine, with each other and with the natural environment. Here I examine how the woman priest contributes towards a potential female religious thought and language, and how she particularly stands as a witness to the responsibility of care towards the earth and of redemption from unjust relationships. Chapters 6 and 7 consider the connection between blood and sacrifice, menstruation and misogyny, which have hitherto kept women from holy spaces and rites. I also examine here the notion of self-sacrifice. In the final chapter I offer some reflections from my own and others' experiences, which I hope will ground my arguments in the concrete life of Christian ministry and discipleship. Theology is about making connections between what we hear and do in worship and how we understand ourselves and act in our everyday lives. I hope this book goes some way towards helping us to enrich our understanding of God and of ourselves, and the way that we relate to the world around us. That is doing theology.

2

In the image of God –
the story so far

*'Through him you have created all things from the beginning, and
formed us in your own image'*

Voltaire, the French Enlightenment writer and philosopher, wrote
a line in a poem that translates: 'If God did not exist, it would be
necessary to invent him'. Whatever Voltaire meant at the time –
freedom of religion, civil liberties, an argument for 'rational' religion –
the comment speaks to me about how humans are always bound to
conceive God to some extent as a projection of themselves. And if
some degree of projection is involved, then in a patriarchal culture,
the dominant concept of God is a construct of the male imagination. In this chapter I shall look at how the notion of humans created in the image of God has been interpreted through Christian
history, and at the interrelationship between these various interpretations and a theology of women's priesthood.

Creator God, created humankind

In preparation for Holy Communion, the presiding priest gives
thanks to God over the bread and wine by reciting the Eucharistic
Prayer. It is one of the elements of the liturgy that has been passed
down from some of the earliest forms of Christian worship. The
text of the prayer has developed over time in terms of content and
sequence, but the meaning which the prayer seeks to convey has
remained largely intact. A continuing feature is the acknowledgement given to God who made all things. In the Anglican tradition,
this acknowledgement appears in the Book of Common Prayer
and, latterly, in the text of seven of the eight alternative Eucharistic
Prayers in *Common Worship*.

19

This part of the prayer arcs back to the very beginning of creation. All things take their existence from the creator who formed the universe, breathed life into it and who continues through time to sustain all that has being. God has brought into being a cosmos of infinite order, complexity and particularity. Even one stone, snowflake or air current is not precisely like any other; each individual item is endowed with distinguishing characteristics. As for living creatures, the work of the creator continues in them in the sustaining of life through the process of procreation. With each succeeding generation new life is brought forth that is unique and distinctive in its own identity, experience and potential.

Prayer A (along with Prayers F and G) specifically recalls the creation of humankind. The distinctiveness and potential of the created order culminates in human beings, all of whom, according to the Eucharistic Prayer and the Genesis story to which it alludes, are made in the image of God:

> Then God said, 'Let us make humankind in our image, according to our likeness' . . .
>
> > So God created humankind in his image;
> > in the image of God he created them;
> > male and female he created them.
> >
> > (Gen. 1.26a, 27)

Christian tradition has typically treated these verses as a key biblical affirmation that bears upon the understanding of human life (the modern translation I have quoted here – the New Revised Standard Version – uses the term 'humankind' rather than 'man' so as to reflect the original meaning in this passage of people in general). To be made in God's image – taken usually to mean one's moral, spiritual and intellectual nature – is seen as fundamental, in the Jewish and Christian traditions, to one's self-understanding. The notion of humankind created in God's image is the grounding narrative on which the symbolic identity of the Church is formed, and through which the liturgy informs the identity and experience of the individual and of the community. The notion of ourselves as creatures of God undergirds the symbol and text of the liturgy as priest and congregation re-member the narrative of the Christian faith. It is a notion continually alive to unfolding interpretations and insights. Successive generations have pondered what it means for humans to be formed in the image and likeness of their creator, and what ethical consequences derive from this belief. Hence the virtuous circle continues to turn, whereby belief, understanding and action inform and grow from each other.

God-talk and human identity

To say that we are made in God's image supposes that we have some idea of who God is. And as creatures of God we want to imagine and express our understanding of our creator. Although we know that the nature of God entirely surpasses the limits of human imagination, we inevitably attempt to articulate something about the nature of the divine. The Judaeo-Christian tradition understands God as utterly holy and transcendent, the creator, redeemer and sustainer of the cosmos, who is nevertheless also immanently present in a way which cannot fully be described or comprehended. No human construct can adequately portray or reflect the nature of God. We can only be led by our imagination, which has been nourished by our experience:

> For my thoughts are not your thoughts,
>   nor are your ways my ways, says the LORD.
> For as the heavens are higher that the earth,
>   so are my ways higher than your ways
>   and my thoughts than your thoughts.
>   (Isa. 55.8–9)

The nature of God is mystery, but we harness our perception and imagination in order to catch glimpses of the numinous through divine self-revelation. Such revelation does not do away with the mystery, but strengthens our belief, as it did for Moses who asked to see God's glory and was allowed a fleeting glimpse of God's back passing by (Exod. 33.18–23). Inevitably, as with Moses and his vision of God's back, we have to picture the divine in human terms, since this is the sphere and limit of our human experience. Correspondingly, since we are created in the divine image, we know that something of the nature of humanity can be related to the nature of the divine. For Christians, this is most evident and fully expressed in the incarnation, where God relates to us through the person of Jesus of Nazareth at a particular time and in a particular context. The identity of God is unique and wholly distinct, yet it is in some way echoed by that of human selfhood.

The Genesis story reveals that God imparts selfhood – that strand of identity which is essential and individual to each human being, and which distinguishes humans from other creatures and one person from another. Each individual whom God creates is of a particular race, age, social background and gender. Each bears a particular, embodied personal reality, or selfhood. Each body is unique and precious, one small but sacred pixel within the great text of creation. Our gendered being and function, our sexuality and way of knowing, are bestowed by the creator who made all things and declared them all to be very good (Gen. 1.31). Our human, gendered particularity and distinctiveness are in the divine image – our bodies and minds, the feminine and masculine in all of us, and females as well as males. We come to know something of God through our particular, individual, embodied existence.

Since we are material beings living in the created world, we come to know and understand something of God through our embodied selves – our bodily schemata, our perceptions, our values, our experiences and so on. The way in which we envision God – how we see God with our mind's eye – is necessarily bounded by how we know and experience our embodied selves. Hence, as we become aware of the divine mystery beyond ourselves, we risk restricting the divine to the limited resources of our human imagination. Great artists have tried to articulate their vision of the creator God in paintings and sculptures. We might think of Michelangelo's breathtaking fresco on the ceiling of the Sistine chapel, where God is portrayed in human form giving life to Adam. Although we know intellectually that God is not a human being, probably many of us grew up imagining a majestic elderly man akin to Michelangelo's depiction. In trying to grasp the ungraspable, we tend to limit the nature of God to our capacity to understand it. As with Moses glimpsing God's back, our God-talk uses anthropological terms, in language constrained by the reach of our human consciousness. We believe, after all, in a personal God who loves, speaks, judges, creates, destroys and so on. But this comes with the strong possibility that we will create an idol in the image of humankind which fails to transcend our conception of ultimate reality.

There has always been a tension between imaging God in ways that are so transcendent as to seem a nullity, or so personal as to seem a mere superhuman being. We have also always interpreted our notion of God's image according to the context of our own culture. So, down the ages, theologians – similarly to artists – have applied the notion of humans in the image of God in a variety of ways that have reflected their particular era and cultural background. In the early years of Christianity, the Church Fathers saw reason as the main characteristic which humans share with God. St Augustine argued that reason and will form the primary structural aspect of the soul, the seat of the image of God in humans. He describes a trinitarian structure of this image, reflecting spirit, self-consciousness and love in the human soul and memory, intelligence and will in the psyche. The image of God, for Augustine, orients the person to God in invocation, knowledge and love.

The extent to which sin affects the human likeness to God was a matter of concern to the sixteenth-century Reformers, and differing views evolved among Reformed theologians. Martin Luther, for instance, taught that the image of God is lost through sin so that everything is marred. The lost image, however, can be restored through the Word and the Holy Spirit. Through faith a Christian can imitate the model of Christ as the form of God. Eastern Orthodoxy retained a more lenient view of the effect of sin: the sinful person is still an icon of the divine and never wholly loses the image of God. Confessional traditions may vary in their interpretation of sin and its effect, but sin remains a constant feature in the Christian understanding of human identity. We strive to avoid sin because it hampers our aspiration, in imitation of Christ, towards godliness. Hence our identity as children of God is linked with the obligations of ethical responsibility and accountability. Christians understand each person to be a moral agent with an intrinsic dignity independent of their utility or function, having a duty to protect both the dignity of other people and the wellbeing of creation. In this way, we cooperate with God in order that God's purposes can be actualized.

Since our regard for others is of prime importance – Jesus commands us to love our neighbours as we love ourselves – then the quality of human relationship is of the essence of our faith. Some modern theologians have emphasized the importance of relationship when interpreting the notion of our being in the image of God. Karl Barth, for instance, saw the image of God not so much in intellect or reason but in the relationship between humans and God and between people, most effectively reflected in women and men coming together and bearing children. For John Zizioulas, writing from an Orthodox perspective, being creatures of God is fundamentally an event of communion, a way of relationship with God and with creation.

The divine nature is essentially relational, and the Body of Christ is called to model on earth the qualities of that relationship between the three persons of the Trinity and between God and creation. The triune nature of God and its significance for human relations in God's likeness has hitherto been largely neglected in the Western Church. Over recent years, however, theologians have come to see the Trinity not so much as an abstract mathematical formula but as a model for human community. As humans we are essentially relational beings. From the moment we are conceived we are dependent throughout our intra-uterine life on another human, and from birth our sense of selfhood develops in and through our relations with other people and with God. Christianity is fundamentally a faith of community: we understand ourselves as the Church, made up of many individuals who are members of the Body of Christ. The way we value relationality and community bears upon how we order and care for each other in our society.

How are women in the image of God?

One aspect of relationality that informs our sense of identity is that of sex. Certain qualities and traits have historically been appropriated to one sex or another. Our thinking is pervaded by certain assumptions and expectations about gendered differences. Ancient Greek philosophers made a connection between rationality and masculinity. From the time of Aristotle onwards, (masculinized) reason was set in opposition to (feminized) emotion. Rationality, spirit and masculinity were linked with divinity, while irrationality, bodiliness and femininity were associated with the less godlike animality, nature and earth. These gendered traits were thought to be largely determined by biology. Until the development of microbiology in the seventeenth century, and the discovery of ova as well as sperm, a woman's uterus was regarded simply as the growing medium in which the homunculus, the fully formed human, developed. These gendered categorizations held sway within patriarchal cultures where men predominated in public and sacred roles, kept order, ruled over their dependants and controlled property through paternal lineage. Women were seen not only as less in the likeness of God but also as non-normative, lacking in intelligence, unable to take roles of leadership and subject to male rationality.

Women in pre-Christian societies around the Mediterranean were largely barred from public and religious activities, power and leadership. Male and female roles tended to be sharply defined: the male public sphere, the female domestic one. In the Jewish community women were excluded from Temple duties and confined to their own court. Exclusion from certain cultic and religious practices reflected their subordinate legal status. A synagogue could be constituted only by the presence of at least ten males; women were not counted.

In Athens, women tended to be defined according to their relationship to men – wife, concubine, slave, foreign companion. An Athenian citizen-woman was not usually recognized as a valid witness in court. In Rome, although women were accorded more rights than in Athens, a father had the power of life and death over his wife and children. Although some economic rights for women had increased around the time of Christ, most women remained under the dominance of their husbands. Generations learnt to accept these assumptions as both natural and God-given.

This was the cultural and religious heritage in which Jesus of Nazareth lived and worked. The repercussions of his radical and countercultural teaching and ministry are even now being considered and implemented.

Jesus: a new way of living

Jesus and his disciples formed a community that stood in contrast to the patriarchal culture of contemporary society. They embodied a newly envisioned way of living in relationship that overcame differences such as gender, class, age and race and embraced all peoples into one body. Jesus often paid special attention to the weakest in society, the most vulnerable and subordinate. His teaching and behaviour, within the context of contemporary codes, was sometimes shocking to those around him, even sometimes dismaying his closest followers. He integrated women freely among his students in a way that would have been highly unusual in contemporary culture. He recognized women as recipients, equally with his male disciples, of God's grace.

The original community around Jesus, the archetype for future generations of believers, showed that there was to be no discrimination on grounds of gender any more than on grounds of wealth or rank. Female disciples followed Jesus during his ministry and remained with him at the crucifixion (John 19.25–27). He taught women as well as men (Luke 10.39) and extolled the action of the woman who anointed him with precious oils, an action he interpreted as a signal of his coming burial (Mark 14.3–9). He did not ignore the gentile woman seeking healing for her daughter (Mark 7.25–30). Not did he condemn the woman taken in adultery, but saved her from death (John 8.3–11). His stories included many images that would resonate especially for women – the lost coin, the wedding feast, yeast and bread, the widow. There is no scriptural evidence of his patronizing, devaluing or disregarding women in the way that much modern historical research would suggest is characteristic of his contemporary society.

The 'new way' founded by Jesus overturned traditional concepts of 'otherness' and exclusion that pervaded other contemporary cultures. The early Church inherited the radical message of reconciliation of all things in Christ, and embraced all people regardless of race, rank or sex. There were a number of women among the apostles, co-workers and prophets of the 'new way'. Those mentioned specifically by Paul include Prisca, leader of a house-church and co-worker of Paul (Rom. 16.3); Phoebe, a deacon and patron (Rom. 16.1–2); and Junia, imprisoned with Andronicus and Paul (Rom. 16.7). Yet a tendency towards dualism in the early years never allowed this inclusive ethos to become fully developed in terms of sexual difference. The new attitude towards women modelled by Jesus, and the enhanced role of women modelled by some of the earliest church leaders, soon became eclipsed as the Church reverted to a traditional, patriarchal world-view. Jesus' affirmation of the full personhood, status and potential of women in God's image remained largely ignored, disputed or denied through the greater part of church history.

The woman who anointed Jesus stands perhaps as a marker to the invisibility of most women and much of the feminine in the history of the Church. She performed that prophetic sign-act of pouring precious oils onto Jesus' head. For this she earned the scorn of many present. Despite Jesus foretelling that 'what she has done will . . . be told in remembrance of her' (Mark 14.9), she is not named in the gospel story. What happened in the early years of the Church to dilute and backtrack on the radically inclusive example set by Jesus and his community?

Tensions in the early Church

Shortly after the Gospels took their final form, the early Church developed increasingly patriarchal structures and attitudes – at first sight a surprising turn, when women appeared to have taken a relatively prominent role during and just after Jesus' earthly ministry.

The new community was characterized by the inclusive initiation rite of baptism, open to women and men, boys and girls. In the Christian tradition this took over as the distinguishing imprint of identity from circumcision, the Jewish male-only near equivalent. Circumcision, albeit a sign of consecration in the Jewish community to the service of God, is nevertheless a male practice from which half the community is omitted. It makes sense only in a culture where the male is assumed to be normative and is taken to be representative of both sexes. In contrast, baptism was offered to all believers, regardless of sex or other distinction. So it graphically illustrated the belief, as expressed by Paul in Galatians 3.28, that all people are equal before God without distinction of gender, and that all may receive redemption and be marked by spiritual gifts.

The radical equality between the sexes in baptism may have been further marked by those performing the rite. There is some evidence that, at least until the third century, women performed baptism and were able to act as leaders of worship. The earliest Christian gatherings for worship took place in the home. It was in private dwellings that many baptisms occurred, in women's space where, being confined largely to the domestic arena, women were more able than in public buildings to take an active part. A few years ago I visited the site of an archaeological dig taking place in Bradford on Avon in Wiltshire. Researchers were uncovering the remains of a splendid Roman villa. One of the most intriguing finds, besides the decorative mosaics, was what appeared to be a baptistery let into the floor of the dining-room. By the time this villa was built, perhaps women here were no longer taking leadership roles in their church community. But standing on the site, looking at the sumptuous patterns of the mosaic, the spacious reception rooms and at the commanding position of the building, I found it easy to imagine those pioneering Christian women welcoming fellow believers into their homes. These villas were their own domains where, at least in the early years, they were not only feeding and looking after guests but also teaching, baptizing and leading worship.

New-found freedoms enjoyed by early Christian women were gradually rescinded as an increasingly patriarchal ethos took hold in the Church. By the fourth century, prohibitions were placed on women baptizing, teaching, anointing and healing, and further constraints were applied through succeeding centuries. The early retrenchment may well have been fostered by the tensions felt among the first generations of believers. They were following a religion regarded by contemporary society as not only 'foreign' but countercultural and perhaps anti-establishment. However much the leaders of the early Church espoused the radical inclusivity of their founder, they still felt obliged, for the Church's survival, to accommodate their way of life to prevailing culture and custom. To do this required navigating a finely judged course that often caused tensions and disagreements within the community.

We can see this in the way writers of various Epistles urged congregations to affirm spiritual emancipation and at the same time to heed societal constraints as far as these might lead to social harmony and not contradict matters of faith. So, for instance, 1 Peter includes direction on the submission of wives to their husbands as part of a strategy for the Church's continued existence during difficult times (1 Pet. 3.1–6). The author makes a comparison between subjection to the Lord and subjection by women to their husbands.

The author of Ephesians maintains that 'the husband is head of the wife just as Christ is the head of the church, the body of which he is the Saviour' (Eph. 5.23). The patriarchal marriage tradition is brought alongside the notion of Church as body and Pauline bride-bridegroom imagery. Through the metaphor of head and body, bridegroom and bride, the relationship between Christ and the Church is understood to model the bond of marriage. Here, then, is an example of a cultural tradition (in this case a patriarchal marriage code) being informed and reinforced by a theological paradigm (in this case of subordination and inequality, as in the relationship between the Church and Christ). We can trace the asymmetric nature of the patriarchal marriage code in the Book of Common Prayer. In the liturgy for the Solemnization of Marriage, the bride vows obedience to her husband. This wording is no longer obligatory but is still an option in modern marriage services, and I have known brides who choose to make this vow. Vestiges of this code are still apparent today in current wedding customs. Many brides, for example, keep to the custom of being 'given away' by their father, as if they were a male possession (and indeed they would have been treated as such in past years).

Church teaching through the ages consistently followed the assumption that the patriarchal model of marriage, in which the wife is basically the property of her husband, is divinely ordained. I have in my office a set of commentaries on the New Testament written by Matthew Henry, a 'minister of the Gospel', in the eighteenth century. Commenting on the headship of husbands mentioned in Ephesians, he reasons that 'God has given the man the pre-eminence and a right to direct and govern by creation; moreover, he has (what he ought to have) a superiority in wisdom and knowledge' (1721 vol. VIII:341). Henry readily takes Christ's headship over the Church as a prescription of the relationship between husband and wife. He does not consider whether the axis of the marriage metaphor springs from a human–divine trajectory, rather than a divine–human one as had always been assumed. In other words Henry, like most other writers, is starting with the particular cultural concept of female subordination and then presenting this to model the relationship between Christ and the Church. A culturally sustained assumption of inequality has been mapped onto the (predominantly male) religious imagination and has taken this as a divinely ordained prescription for the marriage relationship.

At the time the Epistles were written, the first Christians were finding new life and freedom in their chosen faith. At the same time, the leaders of the new Christian community had to contend both with the weight of these cultural expectations and assumptions, and with the question of the viability and stability of their community during difficult times. The Epistles reveal these issues being worked out in practical ministry. In 1 Corinthians, for instance, there is affirmation of equality and freedom for all, and encouragement for believers of both sexes to remain free from the bonds and responsibilities of marriage where appropriate (1 Cor. 7). On the other hand, women's behaviour in marriage and worship is subordinated to the interests of mission, social acceptability and good order – constraints later evolving into forms of subordination that barred women from most leadership roles, except teaching other females. Instructions concerning the behaviour of both men and women show the concern for decency, propriety and order.

Leaders saw the survival of the early Church as of primary importance and as overriding the needs and aspirations of any particular group within it. Later on, these temporary constraints referred to in various letters came to be seen as prescriptive for all time rather than as forming a politically prudent but provisional compromise. Thus the radical message of inclusivity and parity before God inherent in Jesus' ministry and teaching became gradually diluted as the early Church reverted to prevailing contemporary attitudes and customs relating to gender. Women's prominence in the Church became muted as the process continued of adapting Christian traditions to contemporary beliefs about women's inferior status. Within the first Christian century, the expanding Church evolved into a hierarchical, patriarchal institution that increasingly strove to keep women outside the holy and sacred.

Among the Church teachers in the early years of the third century, Tertullian in Carthage taught female submission to male authority; and to the east, in Alexandria, Origen rejected women's public ministry. In contrast to the practice of the earliest believers, women were now explicitly banned from preaching and teaching. Writings that focused on the experiences of women, such as the oracles of female prophets, the *Gospel of Mary Magdalene* and the *Acts of Paul and Thecla*, a story about a woman missionary, were not included in the canon of Scripture.

A woman's femaleness again became associated with defilement, shame and impurity, and further religious codes developed that were based on women's biological functions. The chief route for greater freedom for the Christian woman in the late patristic era was asceticism: the renunciation of the sexual life and of the married state, either through lifelong virginity or following widowhood. Christology, the theology of the person and redeeming ministry of Jesus, became a doctrine of the subjugation of women modelled on patriarchy rather than a doctrine of inclusive liberation and mutuality. The anti-female, anti-body polarity accepted by the Church Fathers became an integral part of Christian theology, despite the radically inclusive ethos of its founder and his first community. Restrictions on the ministry and status of women continued through succeeding centuries, especially as firmer hierarchical church structures developed. The Church's increasing institutionalization lowered women's status and participation, at least partly through the development of an all-male priesthood.

Looking again at old symbol patterns

Jesus of Nazareth, through his teaching and ministry, affirmed that all people, regardless of sex or other distinction, are created in the likeness of God and so are capable of reflecting the divine. We are now coming to work out the consequences of this teaching with regard to the way we acknowledge and act upon sexual difference. One consequence of this, given that women are formed as much as men in the image and likeness of God, is to question how we imagine and talk about God and about ourselves as gendered beings.

Throughout recorded history, in our male-dominated culture, we have been inclined to understand God not only in terms of a person, but also as a man. We reflect on God's nature using metaphors and symbols that intersect in complex ways with images of human – usually male – sexuality. In our traditional religious language, we use mostly male images to reflect on the divine, while female gender is left largely without divine reference. God has been imagined as an idealized projection of masculine identity, leaving women bereft of a divine horizon and hence of a sense of self. Historically, God-talk has tended to be dominated by men and focused on male images of the divine; men have imagined God in their own likeness and gender, leaving women devoid of symbolic space.

Genealogies given in Scripture, as with those of any patriarchal culture, are almost exclusively male, describing a patrilineal descent. Even the genealogy of Jesus Christ is given through the male line of Joseph rather than that of Mary, although Matthew's account does make mention of women who were significant in the line of descent (see Matthew 1.1–16; Luke 3.23–38). The Scriptures were written largely (if not exclusively) by men, and historically the interpreters and teachers of the Scriptures have mostly been men. Male existence is assumed to be the benchmark for all humans and for Christian history. Traditional hymnology and liturgy abound in androcentric images, including military metaphors about war, victory, marching, fighting and armour. Language alluding to hierarchy – royalty, kingship, dominion – is also prominent. So are words to do with power, such as omnipotence, strength and might. The fatherhood of God is celebrated in countless hymns and prayers. All these descriptions of God strive to reflect something of the indescribable divine. But this traditional God-talk speaks mostly from a male point of view, being inspired by largely male qualities such as physical prowess, strength and greatness. Thus the male-dominated language and actions of worship reinforce a masculine experience and way of knowing, leaving women deprived of a language and of a desire appropriate to women.

Throughout Christian history, God has been seen as the omnipotent male ruler of his household, the world. His chosen community is his wife or, in the Christian tradition, the Bride of Christ, whom he saves from infidelity and harlotry. Bride/marriage metaphors, used to depict something of the relationship between God and people, make the patriarchal assumption of women as subordinate. In this patriarchal world social systems and cultural symbols are structured hierarchically – male over female, husband over wife, master over servants, father over other members of the family. Patriarchy understands God in terms of these male-centred hierarchical orders, with their low view of women and their assumptions about women's particular proneness to sin. Judaeo-Christian Scriptures have been shaped by the concept of this unequal marriage partnership, and have themselves influenced cultural attitudes towards the status of women, the role of marriage and the relationship between women and men.

The basic premise of sexual difference, articulated in the first creation story, has not been worked through by later interpreters in relation to our being formed in God's likeness. Women's personhood and bodily integrity as people of God can occasionally be found in Scripture: we might think of Deborah, the prophetess and judge, or of Judith, Ruth, Naomi and Esther, as examples of women who extend themselves beyond traditional custom in order to pursue their aims. But the attributes of these figures hardly form a recurring motif.

Rather, women's status is defined by men and subject at all times to men's will, often leaving women voiceless, frequently nameless, and sometimes the focus for sin.

We can see this, for instance, in the description of the breakdown and restoration of a marital relationship in the book of Hosea. Fearing that Israel had become a pagan nation, Hosea became the first prophet in the Hebrew tradition to choose female imagery to depict the faithlessness of Israel in its covenant relationship with God. His prophecies are set in the framework of the story of his marriage to Gomer, a bridal figure who represents Israel; the unhappy marriage is an allegory for the broken relationship between the nation and her husband Yahweh. The effectiveness of the allegory relies on the understanding that women 'belong' to men. Gomer's crime is to allow her body, the property of her husband, to be used by others. Because women are subject to men, they can serve as a metaphor for a community that recognizes its subservient relationship to the divine. Hosea feminizes Israel because the nation is subject to God.

Other instances occur of biblical metaphors of God as the husband of Israel and of the relationship between God and Israel as a marriage. Where these metaphors are used, men – the leading participants in the covenant community – take the role of the bride. In church history, the priest, representative of the Church and historically always male, thus becomes feminized. Women and women's sexuality are excluded from association with God the husband and, where men are symbolically feminized, women are made superfluous and irrelevant. In other situations, feminizing language applied to men or to communities is used as a form of disdain or insult. Such language is applied, for instance, by the author of Lamentations about the sinful Jerusalem. The habit of using feminizing language as an insult remains part of our culture today. A building site or other male-dominated arena will quickly yield examples of bawdy slights that feminize men. One remark I overheard being hurled between two male drivers who were arguing was, 'Do you sit down to pee?' (See Cameron, 1992:107–9 for a list of other insult words referring to the feminine; she notes that there are more words available to insult women than men, especially in sexual terms.)

The story of Gomer's 'harlotry' has until recently been viewed through an exclusively male lens. Commentators have stressed the husband's boundless love without questioning the nature of a man's love which allows his wife to become the object of the male strangers' gaze and sexual abuse. Many feminist commentators conclude that the depiction of women in androcentric texts such as these leaves them simply as objects of the male imagination, desire and disdain. Gomer's treatment, for instance, is depicted in graphic terms. The metaphors of bride and whore, as with many patriarchal images, are fraught with difficulty these days, when we are more sensitive to the recent theological, philosophical and legal developments in the status of women as persons in their own right and of marriage as a partnership of equals. They throw into relief the association of female sexuality with sin – unfaithfulness in Gomer's case, for example, is entirely her own fault. The woman becomes the scapegoat and patriarchy has to look no more deeply at its own injustices. It has ever been thus: men imagine who women are and then treat them accordingly.

Some writers have defended Hosea's treatment of marriage as *only* a metaphor, a fair and meaningful description of our rejection of God's love. Others see passages such as these as problematic, even pornographic, maintaining male dominance and debasing women and female sexual experience. Still others object to the way that the passage seems to condone male violence against women; they argue that the cultural and historical context of these texts is insufficient reason to continue to use them as religious metaphor today. The message of Gomer, they feel, comes at the expense of the real women and children who suffer sexual violence and other forms of abuse.

Hosea's lack of sensitivity to women's integrity and dignity is characteristic of his time. The Judaeo-Christian tradition, dominated by male writers, prophets, teachers and leaders, has developed according to a phallocentric imagination, language and symbolic that has tended to understand the divine and the human from an almost exclusively male viewpoint. Hosea and other men through history have defined the nature and will of woman and of the divine according to man's image and in doing so have found women lacking. Most have supposed that men are more normative than women of humankind and that they more closely resemble the nature of God. It follows that men – and women, too, as subjects of patriarchal culture – have assumed that the masculine reflects the image of God more closely than the feminine.

That Hosea was simply a product of his culture renders him no less complicit in a patriarchal system that legitimized the degradation and alienation of women. Women reading such passages can be put in the position of either accepting their sex as inevitably prone to behaviour worthy of violent punishment, or of seeming to question the judgement and actions of God. Neither the feminine nor the masculine in humanity can be drawn on to describe fully the divine or the human potential to reflect the divine. However, to assume that one gender is closer to the divine and to image the divine largely from the viewpoint of that one gender is to handicap unnecessarily our imagination, our worship, indeed our horizon of selfhood as members of the Body of Christ. This is the situation that has pertained throughout almost the entire history of Christian religion.

God-talk and sexual difference

Ever since humans first developed a spiritual consciousness, we have searched for symbols to signify and articulate our understanding of the divine. These symbols are, by their nature, polysemic: that is, they carry a range of meanings, and these are not always obvious to everyone at all times. Where the imagination is tolerant of new insights, then it is free to pursue an open, dynamic course that adapts to new and revisioned interpretations in its aspiration towards a divine that is beyond representation. Alternatively, the imagination can become turgid and sluggish, like a river whose course is hampered by the build-up of silts. Where only male-centred language is used, the feminine is often excluded or considered only from the male point of view. In this imaginative world, sexual difference is ignored. Thinking about the nature and symbolism of the divine and of ourselves becomes a closed process which resists diversity and innovation.

Symbols for the divine have historically been largely interpreted and developed by powerful, celibate, intellectual males within the institutional hierarchy of the Church. A patriarchal culture privileges masculine traits above female ones in language about people and about God. Women and women's experience are thus doubly subordinated and devalued. The result is that in the material world, women are subordinated, and their dignity as creatures of God is undermined.

Religious thought and language that are biased towards either sex are necessarily hampered by that bias and are non-redemptive for both sexes. Such a bias, as we have seen, has engendered a discordant and unbalanced partnership between the feminine and the masculine, with the result that all people, male and female, have been constrained in their search for spiritual fulfilment as well as in their social relationships. In short, if we really believe that women are fully in God's image, then we should affirm this in our God-talk; and the conviction of our God-talk should be reflected in our worship and liturgy.

To acknowledge sexual difference and to address gender issues in God-talk is no mean task. It involves not simply considering the words we use, but the religious thought processes that drive our thoughts. The entire narrative of our faith, as with the history of our broader culture, is built on a patriarchal symbolic pattern in which dualistic positions of superiority and subservience, autonomy and dependence accorded to the divine–human relationship have been similarly accorded to the relationship between men and women.

There is still no community on earth that has entirely freed itself from the lingering influence of a patriarchal model of power that fails to acknowledge sexual difference. Many Christian women still endure a sense of alienation across the denominational spectrum of the institutional Church. Pastorally, much damage to women has been recorded where 'male' interpretations have been associated with alienation, subjugation and abuse. For instance, women and men who have been damaged by abusing father figures can find the 'male' language of worship deeply uncomfortable. A recent Church of England report acknowledges that masculine imagery in God-talk, including an uncritical emphasis on headship and submission in marriage, has an association with domestic abuse (Archbishops' Council, 2006).

The story of various efforts to bring the feminine into our religious language well illustrates how entrenched we are in traditional male-dominated imagery. In 1988 the Liturgical Commission of the General Synod of the Church of England commissioned a report aimed at counterbalancing the hitherto overwhelmingly male orientation of liturgical language. The report, *Making Women Visible*, noted that: 'For some the use of male terms to include women is offensive to the dignity which women have by creation and baptism' (1988:21). The Commission suggested, among other measures, more inclusive use of pronouns and alternatives to male words (for example 'forebears' rather than 'forefathers'). The subsequent book, *Common Worship*, gave such alternatives using inclusive language: in the confession, for instance, 'fellow men' is replaced by 'neighbour'.

These changes hardly tackled the deep, structural issues in our God-talk that actually can be addressed only by a paradigm shift in church culture. But they were a start, and other writers were suggesting further changes. Mindful that women had few positive, realistic symbols with which to identify, some tried to find images that mined women's way of knowing. In 1984, Margaret Hebblethwaite, in her book *Motherhood and God*, examined God-as-mother metaphors in Scripture and those developed by great teachers such as St Augustine and Mother Julian of Norwich. A few years later, Janet Morley's collection of prayers, *All Desires Known* (1992), leant on women's experiences and on feminine imagery to 'free the imagination to explore the unimaginable ways in which God reaches us' (1998:xi). Several writers (Sallie McFague, Elizabeth Johnson and Sara Maitland among them) explored the idea of God as mother, especially in terms of the birthing of creation and of being born again into faith.

For some, such developments in language were unnecessary, disturbing and threatening. A significant number, for instance, found the God-as-mother image totally unacceptable. A report called *The Motherhood of God*, commissioned for the General Assembly of the Church of Scotland in 1984, was vilified by many church members because it demonstrated the scriptural sanctioning of female and motherly images of God. The Assembly refused even to discuss it. But for others these small but significant steps were liberating and transformative. Some believed that they presaged a radical new era of sexual equality in our religious and social culture. In 1993, for instance, a group of women took a painting entitled *God Giving Birth* to a service in Bristol Cathedral, where they displayed a placard declaring the end of patriarchy. A few years ago, more than a decade after the publication of *Making Women Visible*, I was involved with a low, evangelical church that encouraged collaborative leadership and mission, and generally promoted a 'modern' outlook that aimed to attract people of all ages. The church council decided to print an updated version of their favourite worship songs for use in services. I suggested at a PCC meeting that, in doing so, they might want to consider the language issue and perhaps make some changes or additions so as to acknowledge women's experience and to counterbalance the traditional, overwhelmingly male imagery for God that appears in worship songs. PCC members seemed rather nonplussed. They formed a sub-committee to consider the proposal. At the next PCC meeting the sub-committee advised against any 'tampering' with traditional language. It found no need to look specifically for songs that used inclusive language or adopted female imagery. My suggestion, in short, was rejected. One member, a dynamic young woman, commented that she felt privileged to know that Scripture affirmed her as a 'son of God'. By this stage I had lost the heart to ask her whether she might not be equally, if not more, encouraged to be affirmed as a daughter of God. Debate and a good deal of anxiety about inclusive religious language still abound. The *Church Times* recently sported a rash of letters to the Editor on the subject, in the wake of an article criticizing changes in an updated version of *Hymns Old and New*.

To acknowledge sexual difference in our God-talk is not in any way to disparage the traditional terms, such as father, applied to God. Actually, the notion of God as father appears pretty infrequently in the Old Testament. The God of the Exodus is rather the active agent, the law-giver, bearer of the Name without image, the 'I Am' of Yahweh (Exod. 3.14). Israel is the 'chosen' son by a word of designation, not genealogy: it has nothing to do with 'begetting'. Some prophetic texts refer to God as father when they are dealing with an eschatological element, looking forward to the new creation (e.g. Jer. 3.4, 19–20; Isa. 64.8). In the New Testament, the Gospel of Mark has only four references, but the idea of God as father really comes into its own in John's Gospel. Here, where the author is especially concerned about the coming of the new kingdom, we find over a hundred occurrences. God is Father because Jesus is Son; that intimate relationship is what is paramount. Fatherhood, then, is especially associated with the new kingdom in which all people can relate to God as co-heirs of Christ, through the power of the Holy Spirit (Rom. 8.16–17).

We know perfectly well that the notion of God as father is symbolic and that it does not refer to any biological process. We do not have to interpret the notion of divine fatherhood in terms of 'begetting'. However, the image of the patriarchal human father figure has traditionally been mapped onto our image of God. This is the sort of biological essentialism that has been read back from the traditional patriarchal culture in which it originated and projected simplistically onto the first person of the Trinity. Once we understand this, we can see fatherhood as being about the eschatological hope of the new creation in anticipation of which believers aspire to live with one another in loving relationship. My argument, then, is not to do away with traditional metaphors for God, but rather to counterbalance these with other metaphors that relate to women's way of knowing and women's experience. Our image of the divine thus becomes more rich, more valid, and more accessible.

Trinity and a neglected Spirit

The designation of God as Father is key to our notion of the Holy Trinity. Traditionally described as Father, Son and Holy Spirit, the Trinity is essentially a relational notion that can be read as a pattern for human relationships. Over the years, however, it has been interpreted primarily in 'male' terms, even where the Spirit has been designated as 'female', so that feminine aspects of the divine, and women's experience, have largely been overlooked.

The Trinity models a fundamentally relational spirituality, where all are equal and work together in mutual regard. It is a model of co-operation, interdependence and relationship. It signifies openness and hospitality rather than separateness, mutuality rather than domination, and unity in diversity rather than ranking because of difference. Several modern writers have suggested metaphors that emphasize the essentially relational nature of the Trinity. Elizabeth Johnson, for instance, suggests in her book *She Who Is* that metaphors of friendship and wisdom provide an alternative to the traditionally exclusive male imagery and attendant hierarchical patterns of relationship (2002:217). She reminds us, in referring to trinitarian language, of the notion of Sophia, Spirit of Wisdom. In Proverbs (Chapters 1, 8 and 9) Wisdom cries out in the street and at the crossroads, yearning for the well-being of all her creation, offering sound advice and inviting all to eat and drink what she has prepared.

Traditional God-talk is marked by a historical lack of attention to God the Holy Spirit, who has tended to be relegated in male-dominated religious thought to what has been called 'a ghostly whisper' (Wilson-Kastner, 1983:123). The neglect of the Holy Spirit has been attributed by a number of feminist writers to the association of the Spirit with female imagery and experience, which in turn has been linked with the subordination and marginalization of women in the Christian tradition. Women's ministry – perhaps rather like the work of the Spirit – has always been constant and faithful yet largely unnoticed and anonymous. So the Spirit, as with the feminine, comes across as somewhat vague, faceless and mysterious. The Trinity remains predominantly as two 'male' persons, Father and Son, together with an amorphous, 'female' (and possibly rather unequal) third person.

The idea of the Holy Spirit as a shadowy, mysterious figure, possibly imaged as female in contrast to the other two 'male' persons, is in danger of reinforcing traditional sexual stereotypes. Does it, then, support societal norms regarding the feminine, such as notions of surrendering control, submission and subjugation? Or does a new interpretation of the Holy Spirit, seen from the point of view of women's experience, bring to light important notions about the mystery of God and the nature of human community? Johnson has looked at the ways in which the Spirit is mediated to us, among them in loving relationships, in birthing and rearing, in befriending, in groups and communities (2002:125–6). She notes that Hebrew Scripture acknowledges the Spirit as the prime initiator of community, forging the covenantal bonds that form the nation of Israel. She describes how the Spirit continues to be manifest in the life and ministry of Jesus and then in the community of believers, a diverse group who are one in Christ because they are born of the Spirit. In the Spirit-inspired community, mutual love, reciprocity and respect resist domination on grounds of difference. As the Spirit is both essentially free and relational, so in this community freedom and relation are fundamental elements. And as the Spirit is essentially relational, then so is the triune God.

Perichoresis: a pattern for relationality

A number of feminist thinkers have made use of the idea of perichoresis (from the Greek verb *perichōrein*, 'to contain' or 'penetrate') in exploring the relational nature of the triune God and of humankind in the likeness of God. The term was used in the patristic period (the first centuries of the Church) to describe the interrelations of the persons of the Trinity. Perichoresis denotes a complete mutual interpenetration of and by the persons of the Trinity which nonetheless preserves the identity and properties of each member without confusion. It has been applied to the Trinity as a way of describing a dynamic community living in each other.

In our own era, Jürgen Moltmann developed the notion of perichoresis which links together the threeness and the oneness of the Trinity, without reducing or occluding one or the other, and so avoiding subordination (1993:175). A human community that conforms to the divine model would therefore be one where 'people are defined through their relations with one another and in their significance for one another, not in opposition to one another, in terms of power and possession' (1993:198). Revival of the ancient notion of perichoresis, by Moltmann and other theologians, has provided a useful conceptual structure for those interested in retrieving women's experience in God-talk. Perichoresis affirms the complex, dynamic interrelationship between the three persons of the Trinity which itself offers a similar model for God's relation with creation, and for human relations.

The notion of perichoresis is an attractive one for those who resist patriarchal hierarchy and oppressive forms of political and ecclesiastical organization. For Johnson, the metaphor of perichoretic movement evokes the notion of 'three distinct persons living in each other in an exuberant movement of equal relations' (2002:221). As a symbol of relationality, it can model the hope of a community that celebrates diversity and mutuality, and values equality and justice – qualities attributed to the three persons of the Trinity. There is perhaps some danger here of projecting feminist ideals of human interrelatedness, mutuality and unity in diversity back onto the Trinity. There can be no absolute correlation: humankind cannot know God, and the nature of God's oneness is beyond human experience and imagining. Yet there are, I suggest, pointers here, in the way we surmise the three persons of the Trinity to be in relation, for communities of women and men aspiring to live together so that all people can flourish. The vocation of the Church, the Body of Christ, is to reflect the nature of the Trinity in its essential unity and in the perichoretic dance of its diversity. Interpretations of the

Trinity as essentially interrelational, equal and perichoretic call into question traditional patterns of domination and subordination that have characterized so much human activity.

The pattern offered by the Trinity is one of essential interrelatedness, which at the same time allows for full personal identity and freedom. It is one by which people can find the space to be, to be in relation, and to attain wholeness and freedom. It is also a pattern that needs to be interpreted in the light of sexual difference. Woman is culturally conditioned to incline towards mutuality and interdependence, but (in contrast to man) has lacked autonomy. The feminine has tended to be associated with interrelatedness, while historically women have lacked the means to full self-identity and social power (the notion of women's self-identity and self-denial is further developed in Chapters 6 and 7). Both community and autonomy are modelled in the perichoretic Trinity, and both are essential where all people, of both sexes, are to flourish. The notion of perichoresis affirms that the urge to become oneself need not mean the repudiation of connectedness. It emphasizes both the essential interrelatedness of the three persons as well their full identity and freedom.

Loving, mutual relationships can embrace difference; and a fundamental form of difference is that of sexed incarnations of being in the image of God. This needs to be recognized in our God-talk, and hence in our language, worship, ritual and ways of being in community. The judicious and sensitive use of inclusive designations for the trinitarian God marks one small step away from the traditional social construct of God in the male image. It goes some way, also, towards recognizing that the divine is mediated not solely through the male being but through each person's embodied, gendered nature.

Although, as I have shown, some steps have been made in this direction, many still see the Church as denying women's full humanity, experience, value and potential. For these people in particular, can those traditional parts of the Christian narrative such as the metaphor of Hebrew marriage or the redeemed bride subordinate to her husband be helpful in imaging the human relationship to God? Are they edifying today when women are only just beginning to gain parity as full members of the Body of Christ in the sense of being acknowledged as representing the divine, of entering the holy spaces and of exercising leadership and authority? Are these images so burdened with adverse connotations that they deplete rather than enrich the notion of the Body of Christ when represented by the woman priest? These are the questions I tackle next.

3

In the image of God –
the woman priest

*'Through him you have created all things from the beginning, and
formed us in your own image'*

At the time when I was testing my vocation to the priesthood I was
serving as a part-time prison chaplain. The day that I finally received a letter telling me that I had been selected for ordination
training was one of my 'prison' days. The first person I met on the
wings was a prison visitor and a lay Reader, whom I had known for
some time. Sharing with him the reason for my elation, I exclaimed,
'Isn't that good news?' 'No,' he replied with some consternation,
'I don't think that's good news at all.' Reflecting, as I continued my
rounds, on my colleague's reaction, it struck me as a prophetic sign
of other people's discomfort which I would have to live with as I
followed the course to which I believed God had called me. To become a priest may to some, in today's secular environment, appear
rather whacky. To become a female priest risks not simply a quizzical
raised eyebrow from the disinterested, but occasional unease, dismay,
and even hostility from within one's own family of faith. What is it
about the idea of women's priesthood that causes such a dichotomy
of reactions, from delighted acceptance to bitter opposition?

The woman priest and sexual difference

Our culture has been undergirded by a masculinist way of thinking that has ignored sexual difference. In Christianity through the
ages, religious thought has been dominated by a central male principle that has interpreted a notion of God in the image of man.
In this realm, woman is the binary opposite, bereft of any symbolic
space to occupy, since language offers only masculine concepts of
being. So woman has been left without a sense of self, exiled to an

identity-less blind spot caused by the denial of sexual difference, with no language or reference to her own experience.

This has been the case not only in the Church but in wider society; but where gender meets religion, attitudes and assumptions around sex and gender are particularly trenchant. They impose on women and men a range of gendered qualities, definitions and limitations appropriated to one sex or another. Thus individuals of both sexes are subject to cultural expectations derived from a generalized understanding of the feminine and the masculine. We all live day by day with these sorts of expectations, and even when we become conscious of them and find them restrictive or invalid, we probably decide that life is too short to challenge every one of them. My husband, when I am away, sometimes gets invited by kind parishioners to meals. Being a good cook, he feels a sting of irritation at the assumption that as a man he must be helpless in the kitchen. My response is that he should count himself lucky. I might be a priest, but as a woman I must, by the logic of gender stereotyping, also be fully domesticated, so when he goes away and I am home alone, parishioners do not seem to feel the same need to feed me.

Sometimes, these generalized cultural expectations have more serious implications. Where they are applied to religious tradition, they have limited the role and potential of women, discouraging their own way of knowing and pressuring them to imitate men rather than to bring their own particular experience, wisdom and presence. It was not so long ago that wives were expected, for instance, simply to adopt the views of their husbands on matters of any import. I can recall, as a member of a rather respectable and middle-class suburban church in the 1980s, when for the first time a woman elected to the PCC was also the wife of a standing member. Her husband raised concerns about the validity of both of them serving together, since, in his view, his wife was bound always to follow his views whenever a vote was taken.

Priests, as with everyone else, are subject to cultural assumptions about gender. All people, according to Christian doctrine, are God's creatures. But we have seen that in male-dominated society, the masculine is assumed to more closely reflect the divine than the feminine, leaving women less godlike, subordinate in culture and lacking in divine reference. With the ordination of women priests, clergy and congregations are now faced – at least at an unconscious level – with an apparent anomaly. Woman is traditionally associated with the nature and earth, with the non-rational and emotional, the material and the corporeal. She is seen as the binary opposite of man, who is associated with reason and intelligence, with rationality and strength, with power and prowess. In patriarchal society men rule and control: women are subordinate and carry less authority. Priests are meant to represent God and Christ to the Church and to the whole community, and to represent them before God and Christ. But how can a woman be such a representative? How can she represent the utterly transcendent divine, the omnipotent Godhead, at the same time as being that sex which is essentialized as less godlike, more of the earth than of the spirit?

Where the male is essentially ascendant in imaging the divine, then it makes sense that men must have the monopoly over holy spaces and rituals, religious language and liturgy. By this logic only the male priest can function in the person of Christ. Hence the priesthood has served to perpetuate an essentialist paradigm within which only maleness is associated with divinity, and men only are able to mediate sacramental grace and to fulfil the ministry of incarnating Christ for the priesthood of the whole Church. Ordination of women to the priesthood has brought about a collision of symbolic meanings that may seem irreconcilable. Indeed, one response is a rejection of the validity of women's priesthood – and this, of course, has been the situation for almost the entire life of the Church.

Transforming the religious imagination

If women's priesthood is in fact valid, then the collision of symbolic meanings it brings about must in some way be reconcilable. A woman told me that the first time she had heard a female priest reciting the Eucharistic Prayer it had seemed strange and uncomfortable; she felt it was somehow 'wrong'. At the time, this woman was herself considering a call to ordination. She is now the vicar of a parish in Wales – having reconciled, I presume, the collision of symbolic associations that she experienced. Such collisions involving sex and gender are reconciled, I suggest, through the recognition of sexual difference. When we acknowledge that the male and female carry differently nuanced symbolic associations, then the feminine is free to find symbolic space within the divine, and women are thus afforded divine reference. We can make such a shift in our imagination when we understand the representative nature of priesthood in symbolic rather than literal terms. That is to say that the priest represents Christ not by any natural, biological or physiological resemblance but by a sacramental sign which is a symbol. Just as the Eucharist symbolically signifies the passion of Christ, so the priest symbolically signifies both Christ and the Church.

By avoiding a literal, biological interpretation of the notion of the priest representing Christ we can uncover new potential for the meaning of ministerial priesthood as representative embodiment of the corporate Church. This new symbolic potential is epitomized by the priest presiding at the celebration of the Eucharist, a powerfully resonant affirmation of the inclusive nature of the kingdom and of the Body of Christ. The liturgy affirms that there is no hierarchy among those who receive the body and blood of Jesus Christ; no one stands superior to another at the altar. All, through grace, are equally received as children of God and members of Christ's Body the Church. All believers are welcome at the table, because all in Christ are created and called to the promise of full personhood in the image of God. Reciting the Eucharistic Prayer, the priest on behalf of the universal Church remembers the redeeming work of Christ, and anticipates the final and complete union of Christ the Bridegroom with his Church the Bride. Here the priest makes present the reconciling action of Christ for all creation and represents all members of the Church regardless of any distinction, including gender. Such a reconciliation includes liberation from any state of presumed inferiority by reason of gender, race, class or other difference.

The Eucharist affirms the redemption of all people, women and men alike. Is it not possible, then, within the Eucharist, for women to find a symbolic space for the female to be acknowledged, equally with the male, in God's likeness? I believe this can be done by acknowledging and exploring the principle of difference while simultaneously avoiding any sexual stereotyping or essentialisms. We must maintain the principle of sexual difference as the key for woman to carve out a space for herself where symbolic narratives tell of her way of knowing and her capacity to image the divine. But we need also to recognize the huge range and diversity of feminine experience and expression. Only in this way can our theology reflect truly the concrete lives of all women – the black suburban grandmother as much as the white rural teenager, the full-time housewife and mother as much as the single career woman, the asylum-seeker and the subsistence farmer. The quest, in aspiring towards women's full personhood, if women are to become real, embodied subjects, is to find a purposeful and healing way to respond to sexual difference that allows for this multiplicity. We need a new conceptual framework that does not ignore or impoverish the feminine in all its diversity.

A theology of women's priesthood offers such a framework. It provides us with a route for exploring the transformative potential of sexual difference in the Anglican tradition. A priesthood that includes women cannot ignore sexual difference: so the entire religious way of thinking, in which the priesthood plays an important part, is itself now subject to transformation. The woman priest is a symbolic focus for the sacramentality of the female body, of nature and emotion, indeed of all those elements that have been associated with the feminine when set in opposition to the masculine. To more fully recognize likeness to the divine in the feminine as well as in the masculine is to open up hitherto unknown horizons in our religious thinking. She invites us to consider feminine aspects of the divine and the divine within the feminine. And in doing this, she brings close the possibility of a cultural transformation that will allow women to be equal subjects of culture. In this way, women are afforded identity through an appropriate symbolic representation that mediates the divine through their own embodied nature *as women*. We can now all recognize the divine in the bodily realities of our own human corporeality and sexuality.

With a priesthood that incorporates women, the feminine is finally acknowledged as able to mediate the divine, because it is seen to be a place where God is to be found. Nature, corporeality, emotion and sexuality, all traditionally associated with the feminine, are affirmed in their sacramental significance, and can no longer be ignored or undervalued as less godlike. As the priesthood of both women and men becomes fully accepted and normative, it may be that age-old dualistic interpretations of the image of God (spirit, reason, male above, nature, matter, female below) will be undermined.

Moreover, the divine itself can no longer be seen in terms of sexual polarities: God is both male and female, neither male nor female, and the dynamic is primarily one not of binary opposites but of equality in difference.

The woman priest gives embodied expression to what has previously been ignored, repressed and denied in a masculinist spirituality that has forgotten sexual difference. In other words, she has begun to create a symbolic space for women in the hitherto masculinist symbolic order, and to call for the recognition of and respect for sexed identity proper to each gender. And since she is representative of the Body of Christ, then what she signifies pertains not just to her, but to the entire believing community for whom, through her presence, the feminine religious symbolic is being re-membered and re-enlivened.

As this feminine symbolic space begins to take shape, it is likely that the absurdity of excluding women from the divine becomes ever more evident and less tenable. It will result in new hope for those seeking a kingdom-shaped Church, and new creativity for those seeking valid and meaningful ways to express religious experience. It will also, for some people more than others, produce uncertainty and risk: if traditional religious thinking is destabilized, then so is our own identity as creatures of God. What happens to God-talk and worship when the divine is affirmed as being reflected in the feminine as much as in the masculine? Indeed, how can the divine be approached in terms of women's bodiliness and physiological functions? What happens when women and men affirm that God is revealed in those feminine traits in personality and makeup as much as in masculine traits? How can the narratives of faith be reinterpreted with regard to sexual difference and recognition of the feminine within the divine? How should the Church respond to the recognition that it is in the mutuality and reciprocity of female and male that people come to full personhood in the image of God? How does this open up the image of the divine, and of human identity in God's likeness? These are all questions that have surfaced in an explicit way since the ordination of women, whose priesthood calls for a fresh reflection on the identity of the Church and of individual believers. A process of rediscovery of the image of God is not a comfortable journey.

Bringing the feminine into God-talk

Although the presence of the woman priest may herald a trans-formation in religious thinking, we cannot guess what this will look like, because our thinking is grounded in this male-centred, dualistic system. We can be alert to what is missing in the present masculinist symbolic order. We can be sensitive to the collision that occurs between the female priest and current religious symbol and narrative within the context of the Eucharist. But as to the future, we can only imagine the unimaginable in terms of the unthought and the unsymbolized. We cannot predict exactly how the woman priest will change our thinking and language, because what this process might eventually reveal is unknowable. We cannot reliably conjecture on a possible future female symbolic. But we can perhaps speculate that such a symbolic, in privileging difference, will continue to play on the fluidity of sexual imagery around the divine and the Church, and will draw on corporeal and maternal signifiers of the divine associated with the feminine.

The female priest brings to corporeal reality the feminine mater-nal symbols that have been lacking in a male-only priesthood. Thus she inaugurates in bodily form a revolution in religious thought and practice that has hitherto been limited to philosophical and theological discourse. She symbolizes God (who is both and neither male and female, father, mother and son) and the Church, variously symbolized as both bride, body and mother. At the same time she affirms the sacramental significance of the female body and invites consideration of symbols associated with it – mother, bride, whore and so on. The woman priest hence opens up a reading of feminine aspects of the divine and of humankind within Christian faith narratives. And in doing so, she helps to uncover the latent begin-nings of a female religious symbolic. These beginnings do not have to be invented; they already exist, but have been under-explored. For instance, images of the maternal divine are present in Scripture, but they have not been highly developed. There has been little incentive to do so in the historically masculinist environment of Protestantism. In Roman Catholicism, maternal imagery has tended to focus around the Virgin Mary and the maternal divine can be medi-ated only through an exclusively male priesthood.

By exploring metaphors associated with the feminine, women can be affirmed as valid mediators of the divine image. Those characteristics traditionally associated more with women should be (and increasingly are) valued and celebrated, albeit alongside other male ones (the knight and dragon-slayer, say) that women may in the past have learnt on the whole to avoid. Perhaps there is a danger here that, in seeking women's selfhood through feminine aspects of the divine, women might aspire only to those characteristics that have traditionally been associated with the feminine. Parents bringing babies for baptism have told me that they are glad to have a female minister because it seems more 'natural' to see a motherly figure holding an infant. This could be read as an example of sexual stereotyping – categorizing the feminine according to traditional assumptions. On the other hand, is not a woman cradling a child still an excellent (though not exhaustive) symbol of our loving, nurturing God?

God-talk refers ultimately to what is not known, so gendered analogies are of course only ever symbolic. The symbols with which we are familiar are themselves unstable and fluid. There are scriptural metaphors and similes for God as midwife and carer (Isa. 66.7–9, 13) as well as king and husband (Ps. 45.6; Song of Songs 5.1). The point here is not to slot symbols into dualistic categories traditionally associated with one sex or another. It is rather to value difference and diversity in a way that has hitherto not been possible in an exclusively male ecclesiastical hierarchy. When we use symbolism associated with the feminine in our God-talk, then certain aspects of the divine come sharply into focus. Many of these can be grouped around the notion of natality which I introduced in Chapter 1.

Women's experiences of giving birth have historically been under-explored as a resource for theology, but this essentially female function, now bodily represented by the woman priest, clearly symbolizes aspects of the divine. This is not to imply that women who do not possess a womb or who have not given birth or do not want to become mothers are somehow lacking in perceived feminine traits. Assumptions about what is feminine and about motherhood have so far largely been shaped by male thought. Moreover, those who are mothers have not all shared a common experience. A woman's relationship to childbirth is shaped by discourses of gender, reproduction, maternity, technology and so on, and is not simply biologically defined. The womb in this context is not used simply to describe an organ that nurtures a foetus to full term, but a symbol of God's creative power. Beside this, every living person has been born of a woman, has started life in a womb and has survived the passage to birth. So, although we do not remember our intrauterine life, the womb carries weighty symbolic significance.

Maternal divine images

The natural seasons and intimacy with regeneration associated with the womb are prolific in connotations of God's self-revelation through the rhythms of the created cosmos. The psalmist praises this creator God who bids all living things flourish according to seasons governed by the sun and moon (Ps. 104); and the writer of Ecclesiastes teaches that all people are subject to the times and seasons that God has determined (Eccles. 3). Women's monthly reproductive cycle bears God's image; it chimes with other rhythms in creation which are all signifiers of God's creativity. The creator and sustainer God is the God of fecundity and creative potential, who forges and brings forth an infinite succession of new life in the material cosmos. Creation is not a once-for-all-time, single event but an ongoing process through which God sustains the living world by giving life to each succeeding generation of creatures. Women embody these divine procreative qualities in their generative power, bringing each new generation to birth in a continual cycle of procreation.

The womb, the primal place in which we become body, is the human crucible of new life. It offers an eloquent image of God who nurtures life and brings to birth. The still and patient God has waited through aeons while the earth nurtures new life in the evolution of ever more intricately and finely balanced ecosystems that are in tune with every fluctuation of the earth's atmosphere and climates. Similarly, the pregnant woman experiences the stillness and patience of the long period of waiting-time, as her body nourishes the embryo into life and vigour. We might also fruitfully link the time of pregnancy with the waiting in prayer for the Lord, and the similar attendant feelings of yearning, humility, acceptance, perhaps also alienation and protest. The woman waiting in expectation for the birth of her child becomes a vivid metaphor for the whole cosmos, the body of God, groaning in labour as it anticipates the birth of the new heaven and new earth (Rom. 8.22; Rev. 21.1).

The intimate love and care evident in this image is an ancient theme. There are many instances of authors in Scripture making an association between the womb and the love a mother has for her child, and linking this with God's love for humankind. The Hebrew words for 'womb' (*rehem*) and for God's compassion or covenant love (*rahamim*) come from the same verb, 'to have compassion' *(rhm)*. Of course, compassion is a trait not confined exclusively to the feminine. Neither does this trait exclude other contrasting traits, often traditionally thought of as 'unfeminine'. Nevertheless, references to God's mercy using this derivation – there are thirteen in the Old Testament – carry a connotation of motherly love, and so are inherently associated with the feminine. Jonah, for example, speaks of God as 'gracious and merciful' (4.2), as does the psalmist (Ps. 86.15).

The passage from the womb into the world reflects the process of new birth experienced by all who become members of the Body of Christ. Jesus uses the powerful metaphor of people being born again to depict their entry into the life of faith (John 3.3). Indeed, in the rite of baptism, as a baby emerges from the waters of the womb to take its first breath, so the neophyte emerges from water to signify entry into their new life in Christ. The narrative repeated at every Eucharist proclaims that Jesus reveals God to the world, and reconciles the world to God. So as all human beings image the divine, all of us, through Christ, can be reconciled to our creator through the gift of new birth in Christ. And all church members, priest and people alike, are 'mothers' in nurturing others to new life in Christ. Similarly, the pregnant mother nurtures and sustains the growing foetus until the moment of birth into the world.

The moment of new birth for the Christian comes about only through the suffering and death of Christ, who endured crucifixion so that the Church might be born. For any pregnant mother, birth is potentially a hazardous time that involves a degree of suffering and the risk of her own death for the sake of her child. Bringing forth new life is costly, yet with a successful delivery, agony is over-taken by joy. Jesus used the notion of a woman's journey through pain to joy during the birth of her child as a simile for the transition his disciples would experience after his resurrection. Their grief over his death would turn to a joy that no worldly event could destroy (John 16.21).

God is the rock, the faithful supporter and friend who never deserts us, who guides us through the 'darkest valley' (Ps. 23.4). The woman in labour knows the value of the midwife and others who stay with her and talk her through the potentially dangerous time of childbirth. How telling that the old English word for such a good friend and supporter, 'godsibb', should have been reduced through subsequent years to 'gossip', the mere idle tattler. The midwife and godsibb stand for the God who is our staunchest friend, who stays by our side through our most painful and dangerous trials. The author of the Third Isaiah pictures Yahweh as the midwife who brings to birth the new nation, Zion's child, after a period of barrenness and bereavement (Isa. 66.7–9). The passage continues with a picture of the new mother nursing and carrying her baby (Isa. 66.11–13), and the author uses these intimate maternal tasks to depict the love and care that Yahweh will give to Jerusalem. The psalmist similarly uses the picture of the weaned child in the embrace of its mother to describe the relationship of love and trust between himself and God (Ps. 131.2).

The new life into which a convert to faith is born is one that brings moments of intense pleasure. Spiritual encounters bring a deeper experience of the self and of the world that are deeply rewarding. There is joy simply in being in the presence of God, and this in turn colours our relationships with others and with the world around us. This inexhaustible pleasure is present between the mother and child as they get to know one another and enjoy each other's company as two separate but intimately connected beings. As with the new believer, the infant learns trust, confidence and self-awareness as her relationship with her mother develops.

New Christians are nourished by the spirit of God as they grow into their new-found faith. The comparison between spiritual food for neophytes and breastmilk for babies is a continuing theme in the history of the Church. Several epistles liken this spiritual nourishment to human milk. Peter writes: 'Like newborn infants, long for the pure spiritual milk, so that by it you may grow into salvation' (1 Pet. 2.2). Benediction of neophytes in Egypt, North Africa and Rome included a chalice with milk and honey, a ritual expression, perhaps, of the image of God as mother. Several patristic writers, including Augustine and Origen, describe Christ as mother. Clement of Alexandria portrays Christ as the milk of the Father, the nursing mother, and as the mother who gives birth to his people on the cross.

In the medieval period there was a renewed enthusiasm for the image of Jesus as mother, for instance in the writings of several twelfth-century male Cistercian monks and, in the fifteenth century, Julian of Norwich (see, for example, Bynum, 1982; Beattie, 2003). Private reflection on the wounded heart of Jesus grew in the seventeenth century to a widely observed practice, giving sustenance to many worshippers. Here is a direct and compelling comparison between the nurturing, maternal God and the role of the mother in sustaining the life of her infant. This association is made explicit in some medieval pictures of Jesus. For example, a painting by Quirizio da Murano entitled *The Saviour* shows Jesus seated, opening a robe to expose a wound located where a nipple would normally be found, and offering a eucharistic wafer to a nun in the order of Poor Clares. The link between the nurturing qualities of God through the Eucharist and that of the mother to her baby is unambiguous.

The trinitarian God of self-giving love cannot be expressed or understood outside the notion of relationality. Similarly, the family of the Church can exist only in community, its members living in loving relationship to God and to one another. We see the primacy of relationship in the bond between mother and child. The mother, very often the bonding force within a family, witnesses to this aspect of the divine. Even in Western societies it is still usually the mother who is the main homemaker and carer, so that she is often the lynchpin of family life and relationships, whatever her particular family makeup might be. It is also usually the mother who is the main carer of the very young.

The mother who feeds and comforts her baby engages in a loving intimacy that precedes the development of spoken language. Before a child ever learns to speak, she has absorbed from her mother the language of the tender touch, the ready smile, the twinkling eye, the soft hand on her skin, the gentle nonsense words that say nothing in particular but convey a relationship of security and love. Is this shared, intimate world of mother and child not an apt image of the relationship between ourselves and the still small voice of God who speaks to us, not only in the noisy and dramatic but, as Elijah

Figure 1 Quirizio da Murano's altarpiece painting of the Saviour (1460–1478), Academy of Venice

discovered, in the quiet whisper (1 Kings 19.12); or, as Jesus demonstrated with Jairus' daughter, in the gentle healing hand (Luke 8.54)? Of course, the mother–child relationship I have described here is an idealized version that is glimpsed in rare moments during the course of exhaustion, irritation, frustration, anxiety and agony that

56

accompanies real parenthood. Lionel Shriver offers an extreme exposition of the darker side of the mother–child relationship in the novel *We Need to Talk About Kevin* (2003). The maternal ideal, discovered in God, is in human maternal relationship always shot through with negative emotions and experiences.

Our religious experience enables us to appreciate personal, deep-rooted values that spring from the recognition of otherness. I become aware of myself as a human being and also of the presence of something other than myself, distinct from me but in some way like myself (such as the quiet whisper that Elijah heard). Through this awareness of the other I come to self-understanding. Like the religious experience, the mother–child relationship is inward and personal, and in both a sense of value is conferred, so that the recipients are given a sense of self-worth. We give back in worship the love that has been gifted to us by the divine. The child similarly learns a sense of her own distinctiveness, otherness and value by the recognition of the other given by her mother.

Language plays a pivotal role in the formation of the unconscious and in the acquisition of sexual identity. The function of the carer, usually the mother, in the formation of identity and of language is crucial. One of the first words a child speaks will be her word for 'mother', and one of the first she understands will be her own name. By endless repetition the mother teaches her child these names, cementing their physical bond in the language of family. The binding power of names is a recurring theme in Scripture: Yahweh tells Moses that he knows him by name (Exod. 13.17); Jesus the shepherd calls his sheep by name, and each sheep knows his voice (John 10.3–4). The shepherd image tells us also of God the protector. The shepherd guards his sheep; likewise, the mother is often the primary protector of her child, first in her womb, then in her arms or on her back, keeping the child out of harm and teaching her about potential dangers. She also clears up a lot of mess – changing nappies, wiping away vomit, cleaning up blood and so on. A woman's caring role often also extends to other members of the family, particularly the sick and the elderly. She is often a teacher, carer and servant to those who depend on her. These roles are all reflective of the God revealed in Jesus, who yearned to embrace Jerusalem like a hen gathering her chicks under her wings (Matt. 23.37) and who took a towel and washed his disciples' feet (John 13.1–11).

A mother's experience of attachment is balanced by her experience of letting go. From the moment the umbilical cord is cut, the bond between mother and child becomes in some ways a journey of separation. In a good, loving relationship there is no unhealthy attachment. Perhaps the old saying about cutting the apron strings is a bowdlerized allusion to the metaphorical severing of the umbilical cord that continues through childhood and into adult life. Growth into maturity as a Christian is described in the Epistles as a weaning from milk to solid food (1 Cor. 3.2; Heb. 5.12). The image of the child severed from the mother's umbilical cord (or apron strings!) speaks too of the need for detachment on the journey of faith. We learn through prayer to detach ourselves from desire of things, even from our attachment to our personal concept of God. As the Jesuit teacher Anthony de Mello puts it: 'Sometimes you have to get rid of "God" in order to find God. Lots of mystics tell us that' (1990:139).

God the rock, the nourisher and supporter is also the God of death and loss. Every fertile woman experiences the potential within her body each month for new life, and the closing of that potential signalled by the blood of menstruation or miscarriage. Her life passage from menarche to menopause and beyond resonates both with loss and also with the birth of new possibilities. The loss of her childhood and the advent of her potential to conceive are powerfully and regularly signalled through the period of her fertility. Scripture reveals God to us through the image of Sophia, the divine wisdom by whom the Lord 'founded the earth' (Prov. 3.19). The mature woman knows not only the loss of generative power but also the potential of growth into the wisdom of the crone.

Human beings are necessarily concerned with relationality, life and nurturing. What, then, can be said when the original blessing of loving, mutual relationship is distorted into oppression, violence and abuse? Jesus bore the curse of otherness in the ultimate abjection of being hanged on a tree (Gal. 3.13). Alienation, humiliation and rejection are suffered in the heart of God incarnate who made himself fully vulnerable to the basest of human nature. Such experiences are part of the history of the feminine, and figure in the treatment of women in Scripture. Dinah, daughter of Leah and Jacob, suffered rape from a man who then purported to love her (Gen. 34).

Tamar had to prostitute herself to her father-in-law in order to gain her rights as a widow (Gen. 38). The two daughters of Lot were offered by their father to be raped by the men of Sodom in order to spare Lot's male visitors the same fate (Gen. 19.8). The patriarchy that has ignored sexual difference and valued dominance and hierarchy above mutuality and connectedness has allowed tragic injustices of exploitation and abuse by the powerful of the weak and vulnerable. Women across the globe tell their own stories of 'otherness'. All too often they are violated and undervalued by societies that treat them as less than fully human.

Jesus, the man of sorrows acquainted with suffering, was not a stranger to desolation; his cry of despair from the cross, repeating words from Psalm 22, tells of an experience of utter abandonment (Matt. 27.46). In Scripture women are many times depicted in a state of grief, abandonment and suffering. Jeremiah portrays the northern kingdom as Rachel weeping over the children she has lost (Jer. 31.15); Jesus tells the daughters of Jerusalem to weep for themselves and for their children in anticipation of the destruction of the Temple (Luke 23.28); female disciples of Jesus follow his body to the tomb (Luke 23.55). A bereaved mother knows the agony of loss and separation that for her has particular association with her own body. Because of their relational way of being, this experience of desolation has been attributed particularly to women (Johnson, 2002:259).

As God knows suffering, God also knows righteous anger on behalf of the alien, the poor, the outcast and the stranger (Ps. 146.9; Mark 11.15–17). In Proverbs and Sirach, the divine Wisdom cries out publicly in anger against the foolish and wicked (Prov. 1.20–33; Ecclus. 27). The Wisdom literature portrays a God who values righteousness above violence (Prov. 3.31–35), pride and arrogance (Prov. 8.13). Many women worldwide express anger against the injustice of otherness – injustice which may be in the form of a lack of parity in health care, education and employment, or in the effects of pornography, or domestic violence. Some have expressed anger about the exploitation of the earth's natural resources and the degradation of wildlife habitats, the result of a dualistic world-view that separates mind and reason from nature and emotion. (I look at issues of social and environmental justice in Chapters 6 and 7.)

Mediating the maternal divine

The images I have described offer rewarding potential for God-talk in the context of birthing, nurturing and other characteristics usually associated with the feminine. Many unfamiliar and underused images of the divine and of the Church, the Body of Christ – centred on nature, bodiliness, maternality – now surface. Collecting these notions together, as I have done here, points up how fecund they are in symbolic potential. Because they excavate the experience of women, they bring to light as yet under-explored resources for our imagination. So they carry transformational implications in the way we understand our God-given identity.

Until recently, female images of the divine in Scripture have received little attention – not surprisingly, since there are fewer of them than male images, and since those creating and interpreting those symbols have largely been men. Now, with the woman priest, we have a concrete symbol who is herself female and who simultaneously represents both God and all people. She affirms the equality of both sexes in the image of God and also the validity of maternal symbolism applied to our understanding of God. She mediates the maternal divine in a particularly immediate way, just as a male priest can readily embody more 'male' metaphors for God, such as father or husband. By this means she offers a space for a feminine symbolic and language that opens up divine horizons not just for women but for men also.

Women's religious experience and desire are validated and fostered by encountering symbolically the maternal divine in worship and prayer. Men's religious thinking can be broadened and deepened, because they are encountering unfamiliar and possibly challenging images and ideas. For instance, a woman presiding at the Eucharist reconnects the Church to the divine within the ordinary and day-to-day. The sacraments have always been of the stuff of ordinary life – basic staple food and drink. But our understandable urge to underline the solemn nature of the Eucharist has led us to create such awe-inspiring buildings, music and ritual that we can be in danger of overlooking the humble origins of the ritual and of the bread and wine, and of the imperative they symbolize to cultivate simplicity and poverty of spirit and to welcome all comers to the table.

The woman priest embodies that earthly connection. In the home, this is traditionally the woman's domain: preparing food, laying the table, feeding the family, washing up. In her corporeality lies a reminder that the sacraments are deeply connected with everyday life. Mothers know the experience of cooking and dishing up a meal for family, then spoon-feeding a toddler and perhaps also running upstairs with a meal for an elderly or infirm relative. What better image of Christian servanthood, ministry and priesthood? And it is an image embodied particularly by the woman priest. She reminds us that we can become aware of God as much in the pregnant mother or housewife as in the husband and father; in the woman seeking justice for a rape victim as much as in the king riding to battle; in the persecuted alien and outcast as much as in the conquering lord and ruler.

A challenge to otherness

As an embodied representative of the feminine, the woman priest affirms that women – and women's bodies – are equally with men revelatory of the divine. She challenges the assumption of the masculine as superior and the feminine as inferior and subordinate – an assumption that has been costly to both women and men. Women suffer the voicelessness of otherness, affording identity to men while themselves lacking such identity. Men suffer from the assumption of masculine normativeness that fails to recognize or embrace sexual difference.

The woman priest begins to break this vicious circle of dualism. Because she affirms that women do indeed mediate the divine, she shows that the 'otherness' of woman is not a divine principle but a human construct. And because she affirms all women as capable of imaging the divine, then she also affirms that this is so for all others who have been regarded as 'other'. So her presence also challenges the assumptions about 'otherness' according to age, race, social status, physical and mental handicap and so on. She testifies that no people are 'other' and that all without exception may stand in the presence of the divine and may approach the holy spaces and objects. Liberated also are all those who have been kept on the wrong side of 'otherness' by the rules of any culturally imposed benchmark. Rowan Williams has argued that the ordained ministry of the Church must 'speak to the Church on behalf of the poor and excluded – and specifically of those whom the Church itself *causes* to be "poor and excluded", to feel devalued, rejected or dehumanised' (1984:23). The woman priest is especially well placed to stand in solidarity not only with fellow women but with others who feel rejected by the Church and by wider society.

As women collectively have suffered the pain of rejection and 'otherness', so the woman priest bears the print of this wound. It has been only a very short time that her calling has been recognized by the Anglican Church. She will know of the numbers of women whose priestly calling until very recently was ignored. She may well have been subject in her own early calling to being overlooked, misunderstood, even ridiculed. She may herself have suffered negative comments and attitudes in her search for affirmation of her calling. In her work she will know that in some ecclesiastical circles she is not welcome. Even where she is openly received, she may find herself treated, in the male-dominated Church hierarchy, as an honorary man rather than as a real woman with a different way of knowing and her own particular feminine attributes and gifts. She will be aware, through her own experience, of other women's lives and ministries being painfully undervalued and possibly rejected.

The woman priest, because of these experiences, is likely to be well placed to relate to the pain in other people. She is thus able to reach out to others who are spiritually impoverished, lost or overlooked, and to empathize with those who have tried to find a place in the Church (and other institutions) but have found its masculinist culture and structures unwelcoming and alienating. She can empathize with those who struggle to feel included within the traditional Church. She may also speak to those who have already left to follow other spiritual routes that more readily address their own desires and ways of knowing. They may recognize through her that there are alternative approaches to imagining and responding to the sacred which have not been available through the masculinist religious thought dominant in traditional God-talk.

Revisiting old symbols

To effectively fulfil the symbolic functions of priesthood, the woman presiding at the Eucharist needs to find her authentic gendered being, her identity, both as a woman and as a priest. And she has to do this in the context of a paucity of historical landmarks or linguistic guidelines, since we do not really know what female subjectivity (or female religious thought) looks like. All we have to go on are assumptions about the feminine generated within a male-dominated culture in order to accommodate and complement the masculine.

This is the case, for example, with symbolism around the nature of the Trinity. The Holy Spirit has traditionally often been associated with the feminine. Like the feminine, it too has remained largely unnoticed and marginalized in the religious imagination. If the Spirit retains any association with feminine imagery, then that imagery now has an embodied representation in the figure of the woman priest, herself a member of that loyal yet largely unacknowledged group. Here is a real, flesh-and-blood woman occupying a symbolic space previously taken solely by men. She is an embodied representation, for example, of Sophia, Spirit of Wisdom, longing for all her creation to flourish and calling all to the table to eat and drink (Prov. 1, 8 and 9). Rather than sustaining a symbolic subordination of the feminine in the (male) Godhead, I suggest she is occupying that space in her own right as representative both of the triune God who is neither male nor female and of all women and men who can, through her, attain full selfhood as children of God.

I have suggested some ways that women's priesthood opens up a hitherto under-explored range of metaphors for articulating the human response to the divine. A further range of possibilities occurs in thinking about God and humankind in terms of community. I looked in the last chapter at the notion of perichoresis (see p. 40) and the qualities of mutuality and relationality present among the three persons of the Holy Trinity. These interrelational qualities are generally associated with the feminine. Christian feminist writing places much weight on the Trinity as a model of relationality, privileging notions of partnership above hierarchy, interdependence above subordination, collaboration above domination.

A growing volume of literature in recent years reporting on gender differences in working practices tends to show that women generally favour collaborative, interactive working methods. On the whole, collaborative processes led by women tend to move more quickly towards shared power and to emphasize human resources. Those led by men tend to focus on positional power and authority, and to emphasize rules and regulations and financial resources. In the Church, research has shown that female clergy favour collaborative and facilitative style of ministry (see, for instance, Thorne, 2000). It is a style now being recognized and sought in ordinands at selection conferences (for more on collaborative ministry see p. 84). In short, women and men tend to adopt different ways of working together in community. And since community is at the heart of the Church, then clergy and lay people, men and women, must learn to work alongside and co-operate with each other in ways that are intimate, meaningful and theologically sound. The woman priest, who is likely to favour a more collaborative approach to ministry, poses a challenge to the rigidly hierarchal structure and non-inclusive practices of the Church. The Church's response, if it is sensitive to sexual difference, will be not to marginalize women's ways of working but to espouse them as broadening the vision and ministry of the Christian community.

Another case for revisiting an ancient symbol is that of the bride metaphor. We have seen (p. 33) how the treatment of Gomer is intended to make a theological point, but that it does so at the expense of real women. Such metaphors can seem forbiddingly problematic today when women are striving to take their full place in society – indeed some commentators prefer to draw a veil over them. This would be the solution if the metaphor continues to be based on the assumption that the feminine is inherently subordinate to the masculine, less theomorphic and more prone to sin. But this assumption can no longer be maintained, because it has been invalidated by women's priesthood: sexual difference has now to be acknowledged and respected. These female images in our religious narrative must now be reinterpreted with a new insight. Gomer and other female bride and whore figures that symbolize the unfaithfulness of God's people reflect the wrong actions of the woman. But they also tell of the unfaithfulness of a culture which allows abuse and violence by the powerful towards females and other vulnerable subordinates to be perpetrated with impunity.

The redeemed bride of Scripture is associated with a state of harlotry and has been subject to punishment which some readers find off-putting because it views the woman solely through the male gaze in a way that is degrading, possibly voyeuristic and even pornographic. The woman priest, by her sex, offers a compelling image of the Church as the Bride of Christ. Because she represents Christ, she challenges the view of women as less godlike, more prone to sin, and worthy of dehumanizing and abusive treatment. It may be tempting, because of these negative connotations, to put aside the image of the bride redeemed from harlotry. But I believe a more constructive approach is to treat the subordinate bride redeemed from harlotry as one of the symbols that can be used to critique entrenched assumptions about sex and gender. To be effective, a symbol must mould both the mind and heart as well as the behaviour of the individual and the community. In offering a particularly compelling image of the Church as the Bride of Christ, the female priest challenges age-old attitudes that have denigrated women. By destabilizing this ancient symbolism, she thus provides the hope of transforming traditional images that are no longer socially effective because they do not represent desires or actions that are acceptable in present-day society.

The redeemed Bride of Christ is at home in her body, prepared and adorned for her husband (Rev. 21.2). The woman priest, representing the Bride and the Body, witnesses to the celebration rather than to the disparagement of human beings as embodied, sensual women and men. She affirms women's bodiliness, spirituality and way of knowing as of equal value to that of men, and equally reflective of the divine. She stands as witness against the harlotry of patriarchy with its denial of the full personhood of women in God's likeness, a denial unfaithful to the original vision and blessing of the Creator. The reclaiming of the Bride by Christ speaks of the redemptive liberation of the female sex from unjust power structures and pejorative symbol systems, into a relationship that affirms women's inclusion and equality in the image of God. She affirms the imperative of working for liberation from structures that promote injustices, deny full human dignity and diminish human well-being. She challenges traditional inequalities of power which have greatly influenced Judaeo-Christian cultures and which still influence relations between the sexes today. The Bride, through the redemptive work of Christ, is liberated from the error of a patriarchal system that has kept women from being treated as whole people and full subjects of culture.

Unity in difference

Priesthood has, since the earliest times, articulated the relationship between the human community and the sacred. Any symbol purporting to manifest the grace of God has to be grounded in God as validly and fully as the human imagination makes possible. If priesthood is to be a true and valid symbol manifesting God's transcendent grace, then it must aspire to portray the image of God as closely as is humanly possible.

A priesthood constituted solely of one sex cannot represent the divine to the extent to which humanity is fully capable. Neither can the male body by itself fully symbolize the feminine. Only a priesthood of two equal genders that recognizes and respects sexual difference can adequately offer the image of unity in difference that represents both the trinitarian God and the Body of Christ. If God is indeed revealed in the feminine as much as in the masculine, then the presence of both these elements is essential in any endeavour to represent or image the divine. Maternal divine images, in partnership with male ones, give expression to sexual difference within the priesthood, and affirm the validity of both sexes as created by God. A priesthood of two sexes which recognizes sexual difference offers an eloquent model of the theomorphic nature of women and men alike. It reflects more validly than a single-sex priesthood the God in whom our gendered identity is founded. It encourages women as much as men to realize through worship something of what it means to be made in the image of the divine. Through the woman priest the feminine is no longer only a projection of the masculine; women can now achieve the status of symbolic recognition and distinctiveness that is not subsumed into the masculine. Women's true selfhood becomes a possibility as symbolic space is found that allows all women to come to speech.

It is wholly right – indeed essential – that the Eucharistic Prayer, offered on behalf of the universal Church, is recited by both female and male priests. Only a priesthood composed of both sexes can fully witness to the God of relation and community, feminine and masculine, women and men alike. Only such a priesthood can represent the universal Church that is Christ's Body and Bride, made up of human beings created in endless diversity and distinctiveness. The male and female priest together represent the whole of the human response to the divine in the reciprocity of the feminine and masculine and all other differences that comprise the embodied personhood of all people, female and male. Women and men serving together as priests witness also to the God-intended relationship between the sexes of mutuality and reciprocity. Neither is dominant or subordinate, neither more or less in God's likeness.

Peter Clark, then an assistant curate, wrote a contribution in 1984 to a book called *Feminine in the Church* which was published amidst lively debate about the possibility of the ordination of women to the priesthood (Furlong, 1984). He spoke of an aching sense of disablement in an ordained ministry that excluded women priests. He felt a lack of women's distinctive contribution, and a conviction, among men as well as women, that 'Where my sister is not, I am not' (1984:181). The all-male priesthood of the time was too limited to truly represent all of society, and failed to meet the deepest needs of all women and men. Since that article was published, the Anglican Church in Britain has had the opportunity, through the recogition of women's priesthood, to acknowledge the integrity and value of all in the Body of Christ. (It's noteworthy that other denominations and other Anglican Churches had already ordained women. There have been female ministers in the Congregational and Unitarian Churches in Britain since World War I; in Hong Kong Li Tim-Oi was priested in 1944; and see further details on pp. 103–104.) The woman priest has allowed for a renewal of women's and men's self-understanding and of their understanding of the divine, of the priesthood and of the Church. This renewal includes at its heart the experience of the Eucharist, where all believers come together in need and fallenness to be fed and inspired. And where the female priest is presiding, there is the public acknowledgement that the feminine is no longer neglected, undervalued or misconstrued. As we look to the Eucharist in our search for wholeness, we are assured – every one of us – that we are all created as equal creatures. Our parity lies not in our sameness but in the range of diversity and difference within our equal standing before God.

In our time and place, the woman who presides at the Eucharist alongside her male colleagues is surely a sign that helps to make the good news of the kingdom accessible to everyone, witnessing as it does to the equality, value and potential of all people in the image of God.

4

Broken body, broken world –
the story so far

'Take, eat; this is my body which is given for you'

I was once travelling through a Spanish-speaking country and found myself in a cathedral while Mass was being celebrated. I speak no Spanish, but it soon became clear to me what part of the liturgy had been reached. The priest's actions – his bodily movements and hand gestures – showed me that he was consecrating the bread and wine while reciting the Eucharistic Prayer. I reflected that very similar rituals and gestures were that day being repeated in many churches of several denominations, and that they could be understood by people all over the world. I want to look here at the symbolic meanings associated with the bread of the Eucharist, and the implications of these meanings for our relationship with God, with each other and with the created world.

The bread we share

The Eucharistic Prayer, having acknowledged God's work of creation and of redemption through Christ's incarnation, now moves on to the institution narrative, which retells the story of the Last Supper. The New Testament provides a number of accounts of Jesus giving himself to his disciples through the blessing and sharing of bread and wine at this meal (Mark 14.22–24; Matt. 26.26–29; Luke 22.17–20; 1 Cor. 11.23–25). They tell of Jesus anticipating his death for the sake of others and initiating a new covenant between God and humankind. In response to Jesus' command, as a memorial of that meal on the night before his death, Christians continue today to share the Eucharist. The institution narrative retells his words and actions. He took the bread and the cup, gave thanks, broke the bread and gave his disciples the bread to eat and wine to drink, telling them to do this 'in remembrance of me' (1 Cor. 11.24, 25). In repeating those simple actions, we remember at the Eucharist the work of Christ in healing the broken relationship between God and human-kind. We unite our worship with the company of heaven and are sent out into the world to fulfil our calling as members of the Body of Christ.

The bread we share at the Eucharist begins as ordinary food, the sort that is an integral part of our day-to-day life. Most of us eat together with others when the opportunity arises, whether at work, at home or on holiday. I found as a chaplain that one of the most poignant aspects I observed about prison life was the absence of shared meals. Prisoners ate their food alone in their own cells. We may sometimes choose to eat alone, but for most of us sharing a meal is one of the pleasures of life; and bread (or another staple) often forms part of that shared meal. So bread in itself can represent table fellowship, that gathering to share a common meal which is an expression of community. The act of sharing food is a focal event in cultures and religions all over the world. As part of Christian worship, it is a fundamental expression of our communal identity and of our relationship with God.

We can trace the history of the ritual shared meal to the biblical account of the Passover on the Feast of Unleavened Bread, which itself holds the memory of the spring festival that marked the sea-son of nature's rebirth. Every family in the Israelite community shared a meal in haste and, when the Lord passed over Egypt, they were spared death because they had signalled their identity by smearing animal blood on their doorposts (Exod. 12.7). Following their escape, God provided the Israelites with manna to eat daily as they wandered in the desert (Exod. 16.13–36). The Passover marked a critical moment in the formation of Israel as a people, and their Exodus from Egypt moulded the liberated slaves, through a covenant relationship with God, into a nation.

Jesus' own Jewish community would have been fully aware of the traditional significance of bread and of table fellowship. Indeed, Jesus made use of these connotations on several occasions. In the Gospel of Matthew he teaches his disciples to pray for daily bread (6.11), thus reminding his followers of their reliance on God for nourishment of both body and spirit. All the Gospels give accounts of Jesus feeding great crowds with a few loaves and fish (Matt.

14.13–21, 15.29–38; Mark 6.30–45, 8.1–9; Luke 9.10–17; John 6.1–13). In John, the crowd, remembering the heavenly manna given to the Israelites, ask him for a sign greater than this (John 6.31). Jesus' response is to declare that he is himself 'the bread of life' (John 6.35) who satisfies the thirst and hunger of all who come to him. The theme of Jesus the bread of life continues throughout the fourth Gospel. As with the grain and the bread made from it, a link is made between death and subsequent life. Shortly before his arrest, Jesus compares himself to the wheat seed that must be buried in the soil before it can produce many seeds (John 12.24).

The notion of Jesus, the bread of life, bringing life and nourishment to his disciples continues with the story of the Last Supper. The disciples would have had in mind the history of the Israelite slaves who, under the leadership of Moses, 'came out of the land of Egypt in great haste' (Deut. 16.3). At this meal, however, a central theme is the future reign of God imaged by an eschatological banquet when those who share in salvation sit down to eat and drink in God's presence. In anticipation of this feast, Jesus proclaims a new deliverance, not just for the Jewish people but for all humankind. In breaking the bread and distributing the wine he foreshadows the giving of himself for the forgiveness of many. Jesus transforms the traditional Passover feast to provide the model for the shared meal that would give identity to the early Church. It anticipates a new relationship with God and with one's neighbour, signalling the fellowship of the future kingdom.

The common meal became for the first followers of the 'new way' the visible proclamation of the Gospel and the call to discipleship to all who participated in it. By the middle of the second century, most Christian communities participated in a commemorative meal as a symbolic sharing of bread and wine. Actions of blessing and sharing were combined with prayers, Scripture readings and a homily by the bishop or presbyter. The Eucharist has continued to be celebrated throughout the history of Christianity in response to Jesus' command to 'Do this in remembrance of me' (Luke 22.19). Since the earliest days the bread of communion has represented the unity of the catholic (i.e., universal) Church and the call to a transformative response. The fraction, the breaking of the bread, expresses the unity in diversity that is the nature of the universal Church. As the bread is broken the community declares its unity as one body, gathered together as scattered grains of wheat form a single loaf.

The bread of the Eucharist signifies not a single people with a particular culture, but a worldwide body of people of very disparate cultures who share a common faith in Christ. The bread of table fellowship is the signal of membership of the Church not through birth and culture but through faith and baptism. Unity and recognition of a new relationship with God are brought to visible expression as worshippers break and share food to bring forth life. Food stands in this context for both sacrifice and for service. Jesus Christ, who was broken on the cross, nourishes the community of believers as they eat the bread and enables them to live a new life in the spirit.

Eucharistic significance: past, future and present

As the Israelites fed on manna during the Exodus, so the Christian community, journeying on towards the kingdom of Christ, now feeds on the bread of the Eucharist. The bread, then, not only takes Christians back through the tradition and history of their faith community. It also signifies the salvation brought about once for all by Christ's incarnation. It is an assurance of God's provision, supplying day-to-day bodily and spiritual needs. The bread of the Eucharist points towards the future, for as we eat and drink we 'proclaim the Lord's death until he comes' (1 Cor. 11.26). So what we celebrate is not only a memorial feast but also a proclamation of what is to come. Besides remembering Jesus' death we also anticipate his coming again and the Church uniting with him in the heavenly kingdom that he has inaugurated. That is the promise we celebrate at the Eucharist, where, as Henri Nouwen has written, 'we are waiting for the Lord, who has already come' (2000:135).

The anticipated heavenly bond between God and the Church, foreshadowed in the Eucharist, is often depicted in Scripture as the wedding banquet. On several occasions the Gospels record Jesus adopting wedding imagery to depict the coming of the kingdom. To his hearers, such imagery would have been familiar from the prophetic writings. In Isaiah 62 and Hosea 2, Israel's restored relationship with the Lord is depicted in terms of a wedding or betrothal. Psalm 45, a royal marriage ode, praises the king on his marriage to a princess. The imagery was applied after the exile to the promised Messiah (the Church later also understood it as a prophecy of the Messiah and so it is appropriately recited on Christmas Eve). In a similar vein, Jesus likens the kingdom of heaven to a king preparing a wedding banquet for his son (Matt. 22.1–14). The invitation to attend is thrown open to all, but those who accept have the responsibility of preparing themselves. In Luke (14.15–24) the emphasis is on the inclusive nature of the kingdom. Those who might be expected to attend decline the invitation, and their places are taken by the outcasts and the rejected.

The responsibility to prepare adequately for the coming kingdom is clear in Jesus' parable of the ten virgins awaiting the bridegroom, for five of them have insufficient oil for their lamps and so cannot accompany him to the banquet (Matt. 25.1–13). In Revelation we also see the coming kingdom vividly portrayed in terms of a wedding banquet. Preparations are made for the guests at the wedding supper of the Lamb (Rev. 19.9). The bride, the new Jerusalem, shines like a precious jewel with the glory of God (Rev. 21.11). She wears fine linen, representing the 'righteous deeds of the saints' (Rev. 19.8).

The feast of the Eucharist is laden with symbolism of the heavenly banquet that marks the ultimate union of Christ and his Church, depicted in Scripture as the bride who appears in the full glory of her wedding raiment to give herself to her Lord. The manna of the Old Testament signifies the bond between Yahweh and the chosen nation, an image closely linked with the feminine, with the land and with a particular national and geographical identity. The bread of the Eucharist, however, symbolizes the bond between Christ and the global body of believers, vastly diverse yet held together by membership of the universal Church. So everyone who accepts the Gospel invitation has the promise and hope of maturing to full personhood in union with Christ. Anticipating that heavenly union, we taste the 'goodness of the word of God and powers of the age to come' (Heb. 6.5) in the bread of life and the cup of blessing.

The idea of the kingdom of God is a recurring theme in the Gospels, suggesting that God's rule will be fully manifested at the end of time (see, for instance, Mark 1.15; Luke 11.20, 17.21, 21.31). The earliest Christians expected Christ's imminent second coming, at the same time recognizing that the reign of God was already manifesting itself. Belief in the pending appearance of the kingdom on earth largely waned but the eschatological vision remained for Christians to transform the world according to the ministry and teaching of Christ. Hence we are called, in sharing the bread of the Eucharist, to imitate Christ in offering our lives in the service of others. So the bread that we share, in marking our Christian identity, signifies not only the long heritage of faith but also the imperative of living the new life in Christ as we anticipate the coming kingdom. In the bread broken and shared lies the imperative to make ready now for that final consummation between the divine and humankind, between Christ the bridegroom and the Church, his heavenly bride. For a Christian, part of the transformational act of partaking in the Eucharist is realizing the need not to be found lacking, as were the foolish virgins, in preparing now to usher in the kingdom of God.

The Church, as the bride preparing for the wedding banquet, anticipates that perfect and harmonious union with the divine made possible through Christ's redeeming action. The priest, in representing the Church, testifies to the meaning and purpose of redemption. At the Eucharist, giving thanks and breaking the bread on behalf of the universal Church, the priest recalls the redemptive work of Jesus Christ, and represents all those who accept the promise of that redemption. The priest stands as a reminder to all redeemed people that we are called to work towards the vision of the kingdom that will be fulfilled in the age to come. The sacrament of the Eucharist, then, takes the most ordinary and everyday elements of life to reveal and express the great themes of the narrative of faith, and to call for individual and communal transformation in response to continuing divine revelation.

There have been many and varied interpretations of the Christian eschatological vision over the ages, and there is inevitably a tension between anticipation of a future beyond time and the reality of the broken world as it is. Many theologians today (especially those writing from a feminist perspective) tend to be concerned not so much with a far-off utopian realm at the end of time, but with the transformation of the concrete world here and now. From this point of view, the ethical imperative facing worshippers at the Eucharist relates not solely to some future age and circumstance but to the daily needs of the present broken world. Another current focus (particularly for feminist analysis) is the way people relate to one another. The eschatological vision includes a return to those harmonious and mutually beneficial relationships, for instance between women and men, and between other groups, for which humankind was originally created. Moreover, since embodied lives cannot be divorced from their sustaining environment, this vision of redemption includes the coming of a harmonious and caring relationship between people and the created world. In a nutshell, such a vision demands that we are to 'do justice, and to love kindness, and to walk humbly with [our] God' (Mic. 6.8).

If our eschatological vision encompasses the imperative to right a broken world, then we will necessarily question and challenge any current ideologies and social structures that are contrary to the prophetic vision of Micah. Hence we must be concerned to address the systematic injustices that pervade society and from which all people need to be redeemed. Redemption calls for a vision of justice, mercy and humility before God that moves humankind closer to the kingdom of Christ that believers are called to anticipate. The bread of the Eucharist symbolizes an eschatological vision of redemption for humankind. In terms of human relationships, there is, we might say, a three-way trajectory: we relate to the divine, to one another and to the created world.

The divine and the natal

We have considered how thought and discourse has tended to assume a masculine selfhood. It has favoured the abstract and spiritual over the concrete and corporeal. At the same time it has undervalued the importance of embodiment and gender. Feminist thinkers, in critiquing the historic tendency to ignore sexual difference, have drawn on elements traditionally associated with the feminine in order to counterbalance or destabilize traditional, masculinist symbols and interpretations that have dominated Christian religion and culture. Grace Jantzen, as we saw in the Introduction, makes a connection between male-dominated cultures and a preponderance of death symbolism. Her project to reverse this tendency entails focusing on birth and life-giving – the notion of natality. The wholeness to which we aspire – the divine horizon – is related to our gendered, embodied nature. Death is associated in the male religious mind with women's bodies, while denial of death and efforts to master it lead to widespread misogyny (1998a:132). Efforts to escape death and the constraints of the body, according to Jantzen, reveal blatant gender and class bias: 'it looks suspiciously as though a good preparation for finding heaven comfortable would be membership of an Oxford senior common room' (1998b:108). Jantzen suggests the possibility of destabilizing the culture of death in order to open up new possibilities for a transformation not dominated by the masculine and traditional binary oppositions such as mind/body and sacred/profane.

Birth is a feminine symbolic, so it has been under-exploited; but it is open to everyone since all people are natals. Birth is, after all, the basis for everyone's existence. We are all born as physical, sexed beings, and so we are necessarily grounded in the concrete. Natality is always materially embodied, gendered, and connected with others and with history. It is always rooted in the material and relational (one cannot be born alone). There can be no disembodied being: it is always rooted in the physical and material. The intention is not to valorize a female way of thinking over a male one. It is, however, to harness the potential of the feminine in the context of human aspiration towards the divine.

The notion of natality underscores the redemptive potential of embracing sexual difference. We must think of redemption not only in terms of escape from death and aspiration towards other worlds but also in the context of our material, embodied human lives and experience. Natality focuses on the needs of the concrete, here-and-now world. We restore our broken relationship with God by attending to the needs of God's broken world as we find it. In the aspiration towards the divine, the focus moves from speculation about life after death to concern with life before death. The process of redemption – of becoming divine – involves being concerned with righting broken relationships in the here and now.

Community and redemption

Christianity is essentially a religion of community, and redemption is concerned not solely with the individual and with personal immortality, but with groups, with relationships between people, and with hope for all in life here and now. It is not only a matter of private morality, but of a right relationship with and a responsibility for the well-being of others. Redemption through Christ requires us to help others (whether individuals or large organizations) in the direction of healing broken relationships. If we have confidence in the power of the eucharistic rite to bring about transformation, to demand a response of action and commitment, then this applies not just to individuals but also to the local and global community. Our response to God's active presence, manifested in the Eucharist, is to live and act in witness to the healing, restorative redemption that Christ has already achieved. Through him the hope of just living is restored so that the opportunity arises to live in right relationship with God, with one another, and with all of creation. Through symbol, narrative and ritual we are affirmed in the Eucharist as creatures in the image of God. That affirmation carries the notion of equality before God. So it must endorse an ethical imperative to oppose any beliefs or actions that fall short of God's purposes by perpetuating injustices that deny human equality and diversity, for instance through domination and oppression of one group by another.

A community of redemption is one where the full humanity of all people is upheld and respected. Working towards such a redemptive community involves eradicating the roots of injustices born of corrupt social systems and ideologies. Where injustices occur, it is often women who are left disadvantaged in terms of status, employment, property, access to health care, education and so on. The world-renowned economist Amartya Sen has shown, for instance, that the ratio of women to men in China and in some other parts of Asia is well below that of Europe, Japan and North America, indicating women's lack of access to medical care, food and social services. The figures also reflect the practice in some regions of female infanticide (Sen, 1990). With scanning during pregnancy now widely available, discrimination against females begins even before birth. Religious leaders, politicians and medical professionals in India, where costly wedding dowries are illegal but still customary in many areas, are currently concerned about the growing trend of aborting female foetuses. The practice has resulted in a marked imbalance between boys and girls.

In patriarchal societies, females are denied full access to the prevailing culture, and so often think of themselves as of little importance, emotionally weak and intellectually inferior. Xinran's book *The Good Women of China* (2003) offers a penetrating insight into the lives of Chinese women before, during and following the Cultural Revolution. Through interviews with women who have never before told their own stories, she chronicles a society in which men's physical abuse of wives and children is widely tolerated; where many poor women lack even the basic diet eaten by men; and where girls in poor communities have to share clothes, since boys are given priority in the distribution of any garments available.

Developed nations in the Christian West are hardly in a position of superiority when it comes to equality in gender relations. The pioneering examples of nineteenth-century English women such as Emily Davies, instrumental in the opening in 1869 of Girton College, Cambridge, the first female university college, throw into relief women's lack of access to education and wider culture in the West until relatively recently. Another ground-breaking figure is a woman who attended Girton, Irene Manton. She became the first female professor and first female head of department at Leeds University, and first (and only) female president of the Linnean Society of London, founded some two hundred years ago to promote the science of natural history. Biographer Barry Leadbetter notes that she attended Girton College at a time (in the 1920s) when 'Cambridge University was the last bastion of male chauvinism', refusing women entry to graduation ceremonies and barring full access to libraries (2004:17). Yet Manton persevered to become a world-renowned botanist with a commitment to women's emancipation.

Prejudice in academia against women survived through the twentieth century. Nuala O'Faolain, columnist for *The Irish Times* and one-time university lecturer, recalls how there were very few women teachers in University College Dublin during the 1960s. A female history lecturer was a better teacher than her male colleagues, but she was a 'nobody' in the politics of the college. Another female lecturer 'had to fight the unequal treatment accorded to single women like herself, compared to the married men who were considered the norm . . . she was constantly embattled. And she never won' (O'Faolain, 1996:83). In the 1970s I was starting a career as a teacher in a primary school in Wiltshire. The headmaster once opined that his married female teaching staff (greatly in the majority) were 'only in the job for the pin-money'.

It has taken a lot of courage, determination and perhaps a certain critical mass of far-sighted people for women in diverse societies and cultural situations to believe themselves capable of flourishing in areas previously denied to them: for instance, by voting, by entering university or parliament, by reaching the top of their profession, or by joining male-dominated institutions.

Human flourishing

The examples I have given above illustrate the wider struggle of women everywhere to find a voice and an identity, and of all marginalized and oppressed people to be liberated from social injustices. Jantzen makes use of the notion of flourishing to describe people finding the freedom and wherewithal to thrive and mature. Flourishing assumes a natural human goodness. It is associated with the goodness of nature, based as it is on the idea of rootedness, growth and blossoming. The psalmist predicts that the righteous will flourish like palm trees (92.12). Israel is the unproductive vineyard that yields only bad fruit (Isa. 5.7). A passage from Hosea illustrates the notion of flourishing as flowing from a restored relationship with God:

> I will be like the dew to Israel;
>   he shall blossom like the lily,
>   he shall strike root like the forests of Lebanon.
> His shoots shall spread out;
>   his beauty shall be like the olive tree,
>   and his fragrance like that of Lebanon.
> They shall again live beneath my shadow,
>   they shall flourish as a garden;
> they shall blossom like the vine,
>   their fragrance shall be like the wine of Lebanon.
>   (Hosea 14.5–6)

Jesus tells the parable of the seed that flourishes when it falls on fertile ground (Matt. 13). He speaks of himself as the true vine, and his followers as its branches (John 15.1–8). Human flourishing, ultimately manifested in Jesus Christ, is rather like the vine and its many branches, in that it requires interconnectedness with other people; it cannot be achieved in isolation. Since the concept of flourishing includes the idea of growth and well-being, it is concerned with bodiliness, with community and with justice for all people, whether on a local or a global scale. Compassion and nurturing love, essential to flourishing, are qualities of God's redemptive nature that are seen time and again in Scripture to be associated with the feminine and in feminine language. The book of Isaiah carries the image of God forming a human being in the womb (Isa. 49.5) and showing compassionate care as does a mother for a child at her breast (Isa. 49.15). God is depicted also as a mother comforting her child (Isa. 66.13) and as the midwife when Zion is in labour (Isa. 66.7–9). Elsewhere, the psalmist pictures Yahweh full of compassion (Ps. 116.5) and motherly care (Ps. 131). In the New Testament, also, the divine compassion in Christ longs to gather the people of Jerusalem as a hen gathers her chicks under her wing (Luke 13.34). Jesus' lament here reveals the compassionate God who yearns not so much to judge the unrighteous as to nurture all people to full humanity under God's all-embracing care.

We can see that the notion of natality links the feminine with goodness and a natural ability to flourish. However, it was traditionally the masculine that was associated with goodness. So in the logic of natality the masculine must now also be linked with nature, since it is from nature that flourishing arises. Thus Jantzen calls into question the age-old dualistic association of the masculine with spirit and goodness and the feminine with nature and sinfulness. (For a detailed examination of the association of the feminine with sinfulness see Chapters 6 and 7.) Flourishing stands in contrast to a traditional patriarchal concept of salvation which sees humanity as corrupt and sinful, and to an individualistic understanding of salvation which can tend to become inward-looking and detached from the concerns of the wider world. In the traditional notion of salvation, God intervenes from outside to save humans from calamity, whereas flourishing conceptualizes the divine source and ground, the immanent divine within people, a premise of creativity rather than of faulty nature.

For many women, the sense of inclusive, liberating community necessary for flourishing has been lacking in the traditional church establishment. Concerned to find or to make a model of community closer to their ideals of equality, mutuality and freedom, some have left the traditional church to form new Christian communities or have abandoned Christianity altogether. The Church has historically upheld and celebrated a notion of community that has actually not been truly communal for all persons. The authors of the Church of England report *Faith in the City*, for example, argue that the Church has failed to offer the world a praxis of community 'at least as often as it has succeeded'. However:

> It is only when the Church itself is sensed to be a community in which all alienation caused by age, gender, race and class is decisively overcome that its mission can begin to be authentic among the millions who feel themselves alienated not only from the Church, but also from society as a whole.
>
> (Archbishop of Canterbury's Commission on Urban Priority Areas, 1985:58)

If the Church is to be a community of fellowship, equality and wholeness, where these patterns of alienation are overcome, then sexual difference must be taken into account because it is fundamental to the human condition. The human way of being, of experiencing the world and of interacting with others is closely associated with gendered being, so whenever people meet together, gender will have a bearing on the character and dynamics of the group.

Relationships in practice

The way in which men and women relate to each other in groups has been of interest to the social sciences. In the past, studies have tended to be carried out largely by men on male subjects, with men's experience used as a benchmark for both men and women. However, with more women entering into scientific research, new insights have been gained into differences between the sexes over a great range of areas. Pioneering research in the field of psychology was published in 1982 by Carol Gilligan, who confirmed sexual difference in the experience of women when she traced the development of morality. Whereas previous (male-based) research focused on notions of law, principle and fairness, Gilligan uncovered a morality, primarily among women, organized around notions of responsibility and care:

> The psychology of women that has consistently been described as distinctive in its greater orientation toward relationships and inter-dependence implies a more contextual mode of judgement and a dif-ferent moral understanding to that of men. Given the differences in women's conceptions of self and morality, women bring to the life cycle a different point of view and order human experience in terms of different priorities. (1982:22)

There is difference, Gilligan concludes, in the way women and men structure relationship, how they understand achievement and affilia-tion, and how they assess the consequence of choice. Sexual differ-ences tend to centre on experiences of attachment and separation. Identity for women is largely defined through relationships of inti-macy and care. The focus of women's moral concern is an ethic of responsibility, 'anchoring the self in a world of relationships and giving rise to activities of care' (1982:132). In terms of social matur-ity, men see danger more often in 'close personal affiliation than in achievement and construe danger to arise from intimacy'. Women, however, see danger in 'impersonal achievement situations and con-stru[e] danger to result from competitive success' (1982:42). This is a difference so profound that psychologists have found it hard to discern or decipher since this shift in the imagery of relationship produces a problem for interpretation that has hitherto been in the male domain. Gilligan suggests that rather than the hierarchy of male imagery, women's imagery is better expressed as a web, a non-hierarchical vision of human connection which 'changes an order of inequality into a structure of interconnection' (1982:62).

Gilligan's findings have since been confirmed by other research. Sheila Durkin Dierks interviewed members of WomenEucharist groups, two of which she had initiated (these are groups of women, mainly Roman Catholics in the USA, who have felt alienated by the sexism they experienced in their churches, and who now meet together in homes to worship). Dierks found that the growing body of data on women's maturation processes shows that interconnec-tion rather than total autonomy is basic to feminine maturity. Women continually value and practise relationship in a way that men do not. For the masculinized world, which privileges autonomy above relationality, maturity is correlated with individualism, and 'has a hard time seeing interconnection and responsibility as maturation also' (1997:137).

In the field of anthropology, Kate Fox notes the difference in English male and female 'bonding' rules when meeting. Women greet each other with a compliment to which the required response involves a self-deprecating denial and a counter-compliment ('Hi! Your hair looks great, I can't wear mine long like you.' 'But mine's too frizzy, yours is lovely and straight.') Men, on the other hand, engage in good-natured competitive banter on anything from favourite beer to politics – what Fox calls the 'Mine is better than yours' game (2004:54).

The scientific findings of Gilligan, Dierks and Fox are borne out in the observations of many writers who note the differences between the way women and men interrelate. For example, Myra Blyth, Director for Relations in the World Council Of Churches, writes of watching survivors of Hurricane Mitch in Nicaragua. The men, she found, displayed anger, hopelessness and bitterness about what they had lost. They were outraged at the injustice, and inclined towards either violence or walking away. The women, on the whole, showed resilience; they set to work 'picking up the pieces of their lives and directing their attention to helping the children and the neighbourhood survive. Walking away is a luxury women cannot afford' (2001:156). Blyth notes similar situations in Yugoslavia, where women were able to create communities and help them survive: 'They somehow recognised and tapped into those qualities that hold people together' (2001:156).

Kathy Galloway, a minister in the Church of Scotland, recalls working with two groups of people, one all-male and the other all-female. She found the modes of working together quite different. The men's working mode was 'critical, dialectical and at times fairly confrontational . . . intellectually rigorous . . . sharp, challenging and demanding' (1995:15). She found the 'high adrenalin factor' initially attractive, but soon began to feel increasingly bruised, since she was finding herself working in ways she did not like about herself. One group member commented to her: 'We men are so bad at taking care of each other' (1995:16). Galloway found the women's group, by contrast, open, vulnerable, ready to share struggles, failures and worries. She noticed their sense of mutual interdependence and need for support, as well as an air of insecurity and a lack of belief among group members, all competent people, in their own abilities and strengths.

Galloway's comments echo the findings of researchers who have studied gender differences at work. These show that women often have but a fragile trust in their own perceptions. Men typically are oriented towards a product-goal, whereby the end justifies the means, while women are more process oriented, whereby the goal can easily change according to need. Problems occur when, as happens in male-dominated systems, women's ways of working together are assumed to be invalid or inferior (Schaef, 1992). Even highly competent females tend to underestimate their own abilities. Women can be helped to develop their own authentic voices where emphasis is given to understanding and collaboration rather than assessment and debate (Belenky, Clinchy, Goldberger, Tarule, 1986).

Applying these findings to women experiencing church, we can see that women entering ministry are faced with a male-dominated hierarchy where masculinist ways of thinking, talking and behaving are taken as the norm. They have to negotiate these norms with all their associated expectations and assumptions about the feminine, and are expected to fit into the roles and behaviours that accord with these norms. If there is a characteristically feminine way of being in relationship, then we might reasonably ask how this might affect the Church's notion of community. For instance, how does women's perceived tendency towards relationality bear upon models of community that best reflect the relational nature of the trinitarian God? Can the Church, in its patterns of relationships, offer a useful model that helps women overcome their long history of self-effacement and low self-esteem and truly achieve full personhood as children of God?

Women and men working together

I looked in Chapters 2 and 3 at the Holy Trinity as a model for human relationship. The trinitarian relationality of God cannot be taken as an exact blueprint for the structure and working of the Church as community. But can a discourse about the trinitarian God move towards one about human relations? How do we bridge that gap between a human society characterized by sin, suffering and conflict and that of the perfect, loving mutuality of the Father, Son and Holy Spirit? One strategy is to start with looking at how the Trinity acts redemptively in entering the imperfect human world.

Human relations can be said to image the trinitarian God only in ways that are appropriate to the fallenness and finitude of humankind. They can only ever aspire towards, rather than directly imitate, the perfect perichoretic unity in diversity of the Trinity (for a discussion of perichoresis see pp. 40–43). With this caveat in mind, I suggest that the way individuals and groups work together can be examined with respect to the example of the Trinity.

An institution modelled on the perichoretic Trinity will not adopt liturgies and pastoral practices that promote oppression of or discrimination against particular individuals or groups. It will, rather, offer an example of inclusiveness, interdependence and collaboration among all its members. This is the type of structure that is now broadly accepted across a range of denominations as a good working model for church communities. Collaborative and facilitative styles of leadership in ministry are currently being propagated in the Anglican Church at diocesan level and are sought in ordinands at selection conferences. Candidates are assessed on their commitment to interdependent ministry, to sensitivity and responsiveness to the community. To this end, there has been an increasing interest recently in collaborative ministry as a way for all members to work together to share their gifts so as to function well as Christ's Body. Collaborative developments have occurred largely as a response to the need for new forms of ministry in the face of social change and financial restrictions. Yet gender has also had a role to play. Hilary Wakeman, a priest and canon, notes that 'the places where the idea of collaborative ministry has been most readily accepted tend to be also the places where the ministry of women has been accepted' (1996:10). Conversely, where the authority of a single male leader is valued (usually either at the high Anglo-Catholic or the low Evangelical end of the church spectrum), there is more likely to be opposition to genuinely collaborative ministry and to women as priests or leaders.

Collaborative ministry involves people working together, using their gifts in a co-operative way that is most effective for the witness and mission of the Church. It is often used to refer specifically to clergy working with laypeople, but I use it here to refer to the practice of women and men (whether ordained or not) working side by side in partnership. Collaboration requires the ability to act both co-operatively as well as independently. It involves a degree of risk-taking as well as being able to 'give and take', to share on the level of ideas, to be self-aware and comfortable with oneself and to be able to relate freely to others as equals. Collaboration is successful when no one member of the group is over-competitive or arrogant, and where each member commits to making a useful contribution.

What has research found about women and men working collaboratively together? Some men have been shown to prefer all-male working environments and have sometimes fought to keep women out of the workplace or treated them as inferior members of the team. I have several times been told by women members of committees that when they make a suggestion at a meeting, they are ignored. When a male colleague repeats the suggestion, he is listened to attentively. A fellow priest and nun told me that she was the first woman to join a particular ecclesiastical working group. At the first meeting she attended, the chairman welcomed the four new members and promptly asked her to make the tea for everyone. No doubt countless women have been put in this type of awkward situation. If they complain, they are viewed as strident, difficult or disruptive. They can be treated as outcasts if they are not prepared to join in with traditional male practices such as sexist chatter. Work practices (exemplified in the workings of the Houses of Parliament and in other male-dominated establishments) are typically defined in masculine terms which are not necessarily applicable to or comfortable for women. One example is that, nearly a hundred years after the appearance of Britain's first women police officers, female employees are still required to wear shirts, trousers and boots and carry firearms designed specifically for men. Women's language is often seen by men as emotional and irrational, and therefore inferior, so that women must either talk naturally and be derided or ignored; or adopt a male style which is seen as rational but unfeminine (H. Bradley, 1995:155). Again, female police officers have been found to defeminize their language and behaviour in order to adapt to their male-dominated working environment (McElhinny, 1995:221).

Women and men have different ways of knowing and of relating, different needs and understandings in terms of identity and relationality. Some of these differences may have their origins in biology, and others in culture. And of course there are huge variations within each sex. Where collaborative processes are well conducted, gender (and other) differences are acknowledged, understood and fully integrated. A church institution adhering to values of inclusiveness, interdependence and collaboration among all members takes full account of all forms of difference in order to live out a principle of unity in diversity.

The created world: an imperative for good stewardship

Having explored the human relationship with the divine and between one person or group and another, I now turn to the relationship between humankind and the created world. As the priest breaks and distributes the bread of the Eucharist, worshippers are reminded that bread, the staple of life, is a token of the gift of God's creation. God is the source of life. The congregation gives thanks to God in the Eucharistic Prayer for the creation of all things and acknowledges God's great love and bounty in providing the cosmos and all that it holds.

Bread is also a reminder that life is sustained through collaborating with nature, including good husbandry of the land and sea. The soil must be tilled and fed with care if it is to remain sufficiently fertile for crops. Since bread is perishable and must be made every day or so, it symbolizes the responsibility to respect and care for the earth if it is to remain productive and supply us with the means of life. So the bread broken and shared at the Eucharist has something to say also about good stewardship of the natural resources provided for us by God. It speaks too of the duty to share justly the resources available. God gives ample raw materials to feed and care for everyone; it is human agency that is responsible for ensuring their proper distribution and use. The ethical dimension of the liturgy is explicit; dependent as it is on the hope of the cross and the kingdom, it requires a response of commitment and action. In the Eucharist, the language of hope, remembering the past and looking to the future, is centred on the breaking of the bread and the response in the form of commitment to God and redemptive engagement with the world.

How can we share the bread of the Eucharist without being mindful of the many who remain hungry? How can we eat the bread without regard for the earth from which the grain flourished? How can we be thankful for the fruit of the earth without remembering

God's creative work in all of life? How can we enjoy it without acknowledging our duty to preserve the earth's fruitfulness for future generations? It is these questions which spring out of the corporate nature of our worship, and remind us of our communal responsibilities as the Body of Christ, which must engage with issues of justice.

A theology that seeks for the flourishing of God's creation embraces a love and concern for the natural world. It demands also a respect for life that calls for action to value and protect all creatures that inhabit the world. Our future depends on the way in which we steward the earth. Hence the imperative voiced by Micah to 'do justice, and to love kindness, and to walk humbly with [our] God' (Mic. 6:8) is essentially concerned with justice for the non-human as well as the human world. A move away from injustice includes addressing harm done to the natural environment: that is, where human activity has led to unnecessary and degrading impacts on natural habitats and wildlife. I cannot acknowledge myself in the image of God, or creation as formed by God, without also acknowledging my duty of care towards creation. Human dignity and the welfare of the natural world are inseparably linked.

The question of stewardship of the natural world has become a crucial one with the rapid development of science and technology, disciplines which have grown exponentially in the western post-Enlightenment period largely without regard to a commensurate duty to care for the earth. Science and technology offered liberation from the religious dogma and superstition that were prevalent in medieval times, but they also brought a sense of alienation from the world. The whole cosmos came to be seen as a mechanistic, impersonal phenomenon devoid of divine guidance or spiritual status. Nature and the universe, previously seen as corrupt, now came to be regarded as something to be 'mastered' and then (following Darwin) as something with no higher purpose, caused by random processes of evolution. The natural world was seen to operate according to mathematical laws that could be deduced and manipulated, and thus exploited for economic gain. Nature was regarded as under the technological control of the human elite. American writer Annie Proulx captures this attitude in her novel *That Old Ace in the Hole*, in which a young man, Moises Harshberger, arrives in Texas in 1879 seeking to make his fortune from cattle ranching. He sets about erecting fences on the land he has acquired: 'in fencing the land a certain balance shifted. Now Harshberger felt that the land was servant to him and it owed him a living, owed him everything he could get from it' (2002:86).

The drive to dominate rather than to collaborate with nature, which often leads to poor stewardship, is not confined to industrialized societies. In the seventeenth and eighteenth centuries, for instance, the people who carved the giant stone heads (moai) on Easter Island so depleted the soil and deforested the land that shortage of food led to dramatic depopulation. But the effects – from overpopulation and famine to labour exploitation, deforestation and pollution – are now, in our global village, more widespread and more threatening.

The high consumption of energy and high levels of waste in the developed world are unsustainable and cannot be extended to other areas without further degradation of the biota (that is, the networks of organisms that inhabit the earth). Mounting levels of debt keep developing nations in poverty and economic instability. Wars rage between nations while their natural resources are continually being depleted. Rising temperatures caused by an increase in 'greenhouse gases' are likely to change the growing patterns of arable crops and to threaten the livelihood of subsistence farmers. Flooding caused by rising temperatures displaces people living on flood plains, especially in poorer areas with no flood alleviation measures in place. River pollution diminishes the biomass of flora and fauna associated with it and threatens the health and lives of those dependent upon it, especially where there is no access to treated water. Damming and water-extraction from rivers cause water shortage for human communities and adverse ecological impacts to wildlife habitats further down the watercourses. Overgrazing can lead to desertification and diminishment of biodiversity. Burning of fossil fuels produces acid rain which has damaged large areas of forest in eastern Europe and has reduced fish stocks in parts of Scandinavia and Canada. Non-sustainable destruction of tropical forests degrades the natural environment, erodes the soil, and deprives those who live in these areas of their homes and livelihood.

Human activity now poses the greatest threat to the survival of certain species and habitats, and indeed of the planet itself. It is those with the greatest wealth and power who often fail to recognize the damage and destruction caused by ignoring our interdependency, since the effects are masked by technology and are remote from modern Western life. Patterns of trade, industry and agriculture are pushing to its limits the regenerative capacity of the earth.

There are evidently connections to be made between the logic of domination by humankind of the earth, and between different human groups, including women and men, rich and poor and so on. In patriarchal societies, women and nature have been treated as subordinate, the property of men and subject to men's will. As well as the land and its associated biomass, it is mostly women and children who suffer from the results of poor stewardship because they are the voiceless, the least powerful and the most vulnerable. Women and children, for instance, are usually the ones to fetch water, and often have long distances to walk to collect it. Thousands of children die each day from diarrhoea caused by lack of access to clean drinking water and health education. Women, as primary carers in poor communities, are often the first to suffer the effects of environmental degradation caused by industrial practices or military activity. Girls still suffer from lack of educational opportunities, despite the fact that investment in girls' education is the single most effective way of reducing poverty. A mending of our relationship with God, with each other and with nature requires people to recognize their dependence on nature and on one another, and to move away from social and cultural systems that dominate and degrade nature and other people. Such a vision impels women and men together to be co-creators with God in bringing about reconciliation between humankind, the world and God.

The imperative to rethink the human relationship with nature has become increasingly urgent as science and technology have become ever more powerful. Such a case was made as early as 1949 by Aldo Leopold in his seminal work *A Sand County Almanac*, in which he calls for the development of an ecological ethic. His call has since been taken up by philosophers and theologians responding and contributing to the growing environmental debate. A quest for 'mastery' of the environment – to the point where the world itself could be destroyed – is these days being challenged by a theology that seeks to collaborate with nature and with humanity, and to allow the earth and all beings to flourish, so that both humanity and nature will survive.

Dominion of the earth

Much of the argument on the association between religion and ecology takes as its starting point the principle of dominion of the earth, the injunction in the creation story that defines the relationship between human beings and the natural environment:

> God blessed them, and God said to them, 'Be fruitful and multiply, and fill the earth and subdue it; and have dominion over the fish of the sea and over the birds of the air and over every living thing that moves upon the earth.' (Gen. 1.28)

Until the 1970s, in the realm of theology, there was barely any discourse relating to this principle: it was absent from the registers of theological dictionaries. In fact, many Christians perpetuated a dualism of humankind and nature, whereby humankind was destined to exploit nature purely for humankind's own ends. The assumption that nature could be possessed, dominated and controlled is now largely accepted to be ill conceived and erroneous; and the Church now promotes the responsibility we have to steward the earth wisely rather than simply to exploit it. Today, Christians of all denominations are joining those voices speaking out against the seemingly inevitable tide of humanity's disastrous rush to dominate nature, and they have been heard with increasing respect.

Aware of humankind's destructive lack of empathy with creation, theologians have recently found fresh insights in the ethic of dominion and the imperative to steward the earth justly. For instance, a statement by the Roman Catholic International Theological Commission, acknowledging the resurgence of interest since Vatican Council II in the doctrine of humanity in the image of God, reaffirms the duty of humans to 'exercise, in God's name, responsible stewardship of the created world' (2004:1). The development (or rediscovery) of such an ethic has led to a revisiting of ancient creation stories that tell of human origins and the need for people to be in relation to each other and to the earth (see, for instance, Ruether, 1985b; Primavesi, 1991). These stories can serve as landmarks in the search to re-member that pre-Fall harmony and intimacy between God and people, people and nature.

The account of the Fall in the Judaeo-Christian creation story can be read as illustrating the consequences of the historic imbalance between people and nature, men and women. Wilful disruption of our intimate relationship with our Creator causes a degradation of the God-given, harmonious relationship between humans and with the created world. The story of the Fall and eviction from Eden tells of an incomplete and dysfunctional relationship, with God, between human groups and between humanity and the earth. This broken relationship is pivotal to the history of humanity. Our overweening desire to play God, to misuse our freedom, to put ourselves first, to dominate the powerless, is inextricably bound up with the competition and distrust that exists between the sexes and with the domination and denigration by one of the other and by both of the earth. The path to redemption entails a righting of the fallen relationship with creation towards an ethic of stewardship that enables all creatures, human and non-human, to flourish.

Creation is part of divine self-giving, and to care for creation is part of the way we respond to God. Our goal, then, must be to live in tune with the universe that God has created, and to share with others God's abundant generosity that we experience in the created world. The human vocation, as part of the redemptive journey, is to right the fallen relationship between humankind and the created world, to liberate the earth and all its creatures from oppressive, unjust, destructive structures, and to enable a transformation towards the wholeness that God intends for all creation.

The connection between ecology and justice is both axiomatic and increasingly urgent in a world which has ignored the demands of justice to meet an ethic of stewardship. Mindful of the dire consequences of poor environmental management, both scientists and theologians are now trying to establish an ecologically sensitive ethic that bears upon human interaction with nature. Many Christian denominations, charities and aid agencies (among them Tearfund and Christian Aid) are appealing for governments to mitigate the impact of climate change on poor people and developing nations. An increasing number of churches mark 'Environment Sunday' (previously 'Conservation Sunday'), usually the first Sunday of June, when issues relating to ecology and stewardship are raised during the service. Parishes who want to become more environmentally aware can use the EcoCongregation environmental programme, available free of charge, the aim of which is to make stewardship a key lifestyle and missionary activity. The programme includes an audit to identify current environmental practice and to develop priorities for action in areas including worship, theology, education and outreach (<http://www.ecocongregation.org>). Wildlife trusts are working in co-operation with parishes to manage their churchyards for wildlife and so to improve their value for conservation and as an amenity for local people.

The created world: worship into practice

During my ordination training, I spent a few weeks staying with a Christian community that aimed to live as self-sufficiently as possible. Every day, the bell rang at noon to summon us from our work in the gardens and fields to the Eucharist. We sat on straw bales around a central, octagonal altar in a little church decorated with hedgerow flowers. The community dog, and sometimes the cat, kept us company. The bread broken and shared came fresh from the kitchen. After worship, we filed through the garden to a lunch we had prepared from our own produce. Life revolved around eating, working and worshipping together. The community articulated the intimate relationship we have with the land but which, in our sophisticated lives, we so easily forget.

Our awareness of nature and our ethical response to our natural environment are bound up with liturgy. We are rightly concerned with things transcendent; but there is a danger in this that we can lose sight of the importance and immediacy of our relationship with the created world. Public worship can make explicit the connection between humankind and the created world. The Eucharist, always and essentially a corporate act, confirms the corporate quality of the Church and of the duty of care towards the earth as part of the redemptive process that reconciles all of creation with the Creator.

Dialogue between religion and ecology has shown up the error of an exclusively anthropocentric ethic that sees the earth simply as a resource for humans, without regard to the earth's intrinsic value. Nature is to be valued, respected and safeguarded, not just for human advancement but in its own right. Recent scientific research has shown how humans, along with other forms of life, are all an integral part of a vastly complex ecosystem, whose interconnections are much more intricate than was ever previously imagined (see, for instance, E. O. Wilson, 1992). Fresh insights in the fields of ecology, botany and biology have shown how dynamic and interdependent are the huge numbers of species and habitats on earth. There is now an understanding of how fragile they are, and how vulnerable to the adverse impact of human activity.

The flourishing of nature and of humankind can take place only where all forms of life, and all types of people, are respected and valued. Flourishing is constrained where the values of love, justice and care for each other are not fully extended to the earth or to non-normative human groups. These groups include women and children, and also others who are discriminated against because of race, class, disability or sexual orientation. One woman who has spent much of her life fighting for justice for both women and for nature is Wangari Maathai. A native of Kenya, she witnessed in her youth the systematic deforestation of her country. Without trees to anchor the topsoil, fertile land turned to desert. Women searching for firewood for cooking were forced to spend hours scavenging for what little wood remained. Convinced that there was a better way to care for land and women, she started planting trees, and taught other women to do the same. Before long her Green Belt Movement took hold, and more and more trees began to cover the land. The women involved grew in confidence as they saw that their labours made a real difference. They realized that they were equal to men and should be treated with respect and dignity.

Maathai herself was intimidated and attacked for initiating these subversive ideas. But she persevered, and in 2004 was awarded the Nobel Peace Prize, having arrested the deforestation of Kenya and improved the status of women. In her acceptance speech she called on leaders to build more fair and just societies, and to give economic justice, equity and ecological integrity greater value than profits at any cost. Hers is a story that demonstrates how, in patriarchal culture, those in power justify exploitation of subordinates and of the land by negating the value of those they use and abuse, while at the same time denying their own dependence on them (Maathai, 2007).

The scientist Vandana Shiva, in her book *Staying Alive: Women, Ecology and Development* (1989), provides an example of trying to live in harmony with nature in culturally hostile environments. Shiva writes from her involvement with women's struggles for survival in India through the 1980s. She questions the status of science and development as benchmarks of progress, and argues that they are actually projects of modern Western patriarchy, with their inherent inequalities of gender, race and class. Shiva traces the rise of a patriarchal science of nature back to the European scientific revolution, which accelerated the ruthless search for raw materials. She lists some of the day-to-day struggles of women, particularly in India, to protect nature from destructive exploitation of women and land. She mentions, among others, the Chipko movement of the peasant women of Garhwal which in the 1970s resisted the commercial exploitation of forest resources in favour of native, ecologically valuable trees that supported local communities.

Generations have for too long prostituted the earth's resources to satisfy human greed. From a Christian perspective, Micah's prophetic call for justice, kindness and humility (Mic. 6.8) must embrace redemption from idolatrous practices that lead to broken human relationships and to potentially disastrous consequences for the planet. The idolatry, in this case, from which the Bride of Christ is redeemed, is that of domination, oppression and injustice, whether by one group of another or by humankind of the earth. The fine linen worn by the Bride of Christ is made up of the 'righteous deeds of the saints' (Rev. 19.8). In this context, these righteous acts comprise the work people do, on the journey towards redemption, to rid the world of dehumanizing ideologies that harm people and all of nature, so that all life can flourish in the way that God intended. In terms of breaking bread in the Eucharist, the remembrance of Christ's body broken for us calls us to strive to heal all that is broken in our relationship with God, with each other and with the earth.

5

Broken body, broken world – the woman priest

'Take, eat; this is my body which is given for you'

I was once looking around an ancient, ruinous Christian monastery set in a remote desert in Egypt. I asked my local guide about some curious features set on the low ceilings of the monks' cells. He explained that hooks were suspended there so that the monks, during their long nights standing in prayer, could tie their hair to them. If they should nod off, they would be jolted awake to continue their vigil. Whether or not this was a fanciful tale told for the benefit of visitors, it bears the flavour of the sort of asceticism practised by a wide range of religions in the pursuit of religious and spiritual goals. Withdrawal from the world to live an ascetic life was a characteristic feature of the early Church, when great numbers of hermits retreated to the deserts of the Middle East. The aim was to 'empty' themselves and to become absorbed into the heart of God who redeems the world. They did this through rigorous discipline of the body and renunciation of certain material, sensual pleasures. But these aims sometimes became influenced by a dualistic tendency that saw spiritual enlightenment as in opposition to the world of the body and of the senses. Following this logic, mortification of the body came to be used as a way of escape from the material world, and the body came to be disregarded or even despised in pursuit of spiritual goals. The influential theology of Manichaeism, for instance, taught that the soul suffered from contact with matter, and that intellect and knowledge were paramount in bringing about salvation. Manichaeans repudiated marriage and maternity as evil because they prolonged the spirit's imprisonment in the body.

A disregard of the body in order to reach an elevated spiritual level has been a strong strand in dualistic religious thought through the centuries. In contrast to this philosophy, I have been arguing that human embodiment, in all its forms, is a prime focus for the human encounter with and aspiration towards the divine. Rather than think of the spiritual journey as one of escape from the bodily and the material, we can make that journey in and through our bodily experience – through the real things of the created world. This more concrete, tangible reading of redemption leads us to be concerned with transformative action in the here and now rather than to fix our gaze solely on the anticipation of immortality. Many feminist writers, who resist thinking in terms of binary opposites, emphasize this down-to-earth notion of redemption by seeking to tackle the injustices of a broken world. From this point of view, it is not about escaping an alien, bodily world, but rather living an authentic, relational life in and through creation. In this chapter I examine whether the priest who is a woman, and whom culture therefore tends to associate with nature, the material and corporeal, can be seen as a symbolic focus for such an embodied and earthed interpretation of the role of the Church, the Bride and Body of Christ.

Humankind and the divine: a question of redemption

I have argued that feminist theologies, earthed as they are in the concrete, broken world, take a rather different approach to redemption from the traditional, historic understanding of human relationships with the divine, with one another and with creation. Are these two approaches – one stressing the transcendent and the other the immanent – in irreconcilable opposition? I think not. As people of faith created in God's likeness we gain our sense of selfhood from God, and it is to the divine that our spiritual journey is directed. But our experience of transcendence is grounded in the immanence of our corporeal life: one is not antithetical to the other. Our desire towards the divine is not contrary to our valuing and enjoying our bodiliness. We can understand spirit and matter, mind and body, the supernatural and the natural, as integrated aspects of God's creation. When we do this, then our anticipation of God's kingdom impels us to share in the healing of human relationships with God, with each other and with the natural world.

Historically, things natural, bodily and material have been associated with woman. The feminine has been regarded as antithetical to the spiritual, the cerebral, the supernatural – qualities associated with man. Hence woman and the feminine have been treated as subordinate to, and less godlike than, man and the masculine. However, in a theology of redemption that values the immanent as mediator of the divine, woman can no longer be considered less theomorphic than man. So woman, together with the concrete and the embodied and those things linked with the feminine, now becomes fully involved in the redemptive process. This theology of redemption takes into account sexual difference because it acknowledges symbolic gender assignations. Sexual difference is key, for similar reasons, to a theology of women's priesthood. Women's priesthood embodies an immanent understanding of redemption because of the earthly symbolic meanings associated with women. And a priesthood of women and men together readily embraces both the immanent and the transcendent trajectory of redemption in a way that a single-sex priesthood cannot.

I have argued that woman is equal to man in God's image, but she is not the same as man. Similarly, a female priest is equal to a male priest in her capacity to act in the person of Christ and to represent the Church, but she is not exactly the same because of the different qualities and values which the feminine and the masculine symbolize. For instance, the woman priest, simply by her sex, carries a weight of symbolic baggage associated with corporeality, earthliness and with the maternal that is different from that of her male colleague. As she blesses and distributes the bread at the Eucharist, she is surely an apt and forceful reminder of the earthly, immanent and urgent aspects of the nature of redemption. The female priest who is aware of the symbolic significance of both sexual difference in general and the (as yet largely unexplored) feminine in particular can potentially harness that awareness. By embodying the feminine she becomes instrumental in renewing and revitalizing the symbolism attached to the divine, to the priesthood and to the Church as the Body of Christ. In this way she encourages and progresses a shift in the Church's understanding of redemption whereby the possibilities of the transcendent are grounded and embodied in, rather than adverse to, the immanent.

This is not to advocate some sort of imposed supremacy of the female religious imagination – indeed, we cannot as yet envisage what this might look like. But the woman priest, particularly one who is aware of sexual difference in relation to the realm of faith, can begin to uncover a fuller representation of the divine and of the Church – and of the relationship between the two – than has ever been possible with a male-only clergy. She is not only a priest who represents the Church, but also a woman who represents women. So, if she is aware of these issues, she can bring to the fore (whether in liturgical or pastoral ministry) maternal aspects of the divine and of personal identity which can nurture other women – and men too – in their growth towards selfhood and spiritual maturity.

Birthing a new language

The woman priest offers a female representation of the divine, and so mediates in her bodiliness those maternal aspects of the divine which have hitherto been overlooked or neglected. As she breaks bread at the altar on behalf of the community she has the potential to express in a particularly resonant way the new life that is offered with a restored relationship between humankind and God. Because her body resonates with maternal symbolism, she facilitates that birth into redemption in which worshippers partake as they share the sacrament at the Eucharist.

With this priestly mediation comes the possibility of the beginnings of feminine religious thought and language that open up a greater range of symbolic meanings that was previously available. In this way she helps women and men, as natals, to explore their identity as children of faith born of the Spirit. And she helps all women to find the opportunity for self-expression in worship, in carving out a space that embraces symbolic associations with the female body, such as childbirth, and female sexuality and bodily functions. Una Kroll, herself a priest and mother, provides an example of this process in her book *Anatomy of Survival*. Here she explains the strong connection she feels between birth and Eucharist. When she is presiding, she writes, she has come to relate the inevitability of the coming of the Holy Spirit with the unstoppable process of giving birth. The Eucharist is, she finds, a participation in birth, articulating Jesus' necessary sacrifice as a 'bleeding to bring birth out of death', similar to the way in which women labour to bring forth new life (2001:118). God nurtures people towards this new life as, through grace, they hear and respond to the message of redemption.

With the transformative potential opened up by women's priest-hood in terms of the symbolic, there are new possibilities also for liturgy. In the past, liturgical services were designed and led solely by men and did not always reflect or cater for women's needs and experiences. Some women, as a result, found their own ways outside official church liturgy to express their ways of knowing and to mark significant occasions in their lives. Women-church, for example, is a movement of women who have felt ignored and starved of appropriate language and symbolic forms in conventional church institutions and who have developed their own communities and forms of worship. These include rites of healing for victims of sexual abuse and for miscarriage, celebrations for young women at puberty and for menopause, and birthing preparation (Ruether, 1985a).

Many women's groups have sprung up across the world where members seek justice and explore spirituality with like-minded female friends. The Fellowship of the Least Coin, for example, is a global, ecumenical women's prayer movement. It allocates funds for tackling such issues as gender justice, educational and health concerns and violence against women. In my own country of Wales is a group called Women Walking Together, loosely affiliated to the Ecumenical Forum Of European Christian Women. These organizations promote ecumenical women's networks that translate spiritual principles of parity and flourishing into practical promotion of social change – for instance, lobbying for legislation against sex trafficking and providing leadership training for women in Eastern Europe.

The advent of women priests provides impetus for the development of language and rituals that commemorate and reflect the experiences of women and articulate aspects of the maternal divine. How those opportunities are taken will depend on growing awareness of these issues, and will vary considerably between different local situations and church traditions. In an evangelical environment, for example, where word takes precedence over ritual, changes to liturgy are often more readily tolerated and encouraged, whereas changes to the language used in God-talk (such as in hymns and prayers) may be suspected of straying from the divinely inspired Word of God. In an Anglo-Catholic environment, where the analogical imagination prevails, ritual tends to conform to long-standing tradition that does not always lend itself to alternative liturgy. Nevertheless, changes have been evident both within and beyond the Anglican Communion. *Celebrating Women*, for instance, is a collection of prayers contributed from the UK and elsewhere, intended to articulate women's perspective and experience. It includes a blessing for a pregnant woman and other prayers inspired by women in Scripture (Ward, Wild and Morley, 1995). The St Hilda Community, founded in 1987 in part to explore more inclusive forms of worship, has published worship material taken from the innovative liturgy that members have developed (St Hilda Community, 1991).

The growth of language and ritual that acknowledge the maternal divine and uphold the feminine does not of course necessitate a female priesthood. Indeed, there are those who despair of current church institutions and who want to see the dismantling of clericalism altogether and the formation of entirely new faith communities free of the old symbolic order of patriarchy. Some women have separated from the Church as institution, stifled and frustrated by its masculinist culture and traditions. But many others have chosen to keep faith with the church of their forebears and to work from within that system. We feel the tension between the constraints and gaps of what presently exists and the possibility of what might be; yet we also value being part of the historic culture of our parent institution, even when at times that institution leaves us bereft and undernourished.

This pioneering dialogue between past and future presents a role that the woman priest is particularly well placed to play. She has by definition placed herself within the established ecclesiastical tradition and hierarchy, yet is also an outsider, unacknowledged in the religious imaginary (see p. 46) and in some ways alien to the clerical culture of the institution and its practices. As a representative of women's experiences and aspirations, she may well have an interest in developing a female religious imaginary and in its expression in new forms of ritual and liturgy. Where the divine mystery is named, symbolized and expressed in terms of the feminine as well as the masculine, then new possibilities for experience of the mystery of God are disclosed. There is much scope for ritual that is transformative in its recognition of sexual difference and hence of the needs, experiences and aspirations of women. Such ritual can be challenging (even scandalous) for some, yet adhere nevertheless to accepted Anglican theology.

Where a theology of priesthood pertains that allows for innovations in symbolic potential, then the woman priest who is aware of the range of issues I have mentioned can help to counterbalance a patriarchal ecclesial structure that has so far been stubbornly blind to the feminine. The principle of sexual difference must be applied to the Church and to all social forms in order for women to achieve a valid spiritual and cultural identity that is proper to them and not simply borrowed from the masculine norm. The woman priest celebrating the Eucharist is taking part in a redemptive act, not least because she is claiming full personhood for all women. She embodies a movement away from injustice – for instance, from abjection and subjugation caused by abusive relationships and practices. She represents a healing of the injustice done to women by the Church itself in failing to recognize women as subjects who are equal in the divine image – a failure marked in male-centred language, insensitive liturgy and excluding, hierarchical structures.

Part of the priestly calling is to the healing of humankind's relationship with God, and that includes addressing a world which has been damaged by its lack of affirmation of sexual difference and by its repression of the feminine. The woman priest throws into relief the error of patriarchy in its fear and subordination of the 'other'. The historic lack of representation of the female divine in the Christian tradition is addressed by the focus of feminine symbolism within the priesthood of women, which promotes the possibility of full selfhood through the birth of feminine religious thought and language.

Women and men hold equal value and responsibility in the work of restoring humanity to the original, harmonious relationship that God intended and that is portrayed in Scripture as the union between Christ the bridegroom and the Church, his Bride. To this end, the female priest offers the hope for a religious symbolic and language that open up divine horizons for all people without exception.

One to another: the call to flourish

I have argued that the woman priest is particularly well placed to embody the notion of natality. All of us are born, but women especially carry the range of symbolic significance associated with birthing and nurturing. In embodying natality as a human condition that is just as powerful as mortality, she gives expression to the call for all natals to flourish in their aspiration towards the divine. Birthing, nurturing and flourishing necessarily require compassionate action. Echoing God's love for humankind, a mother longs to protect and care for her children while allowing them to grow and to flourish into adulthood. The woman priest testifies to the ability of women everywhere to mediate the divine through a celebration of their embodied, gendered, procreative nature. From this flows the promise of flourishing to all people, all natals. The concept of flourishing, symbolized in women's priesthood, requires us to work for God's kingdom by mending the broken relationships that pertain wherever mutuality and equality have been overtaken by domination and subjugation.

If we are to be agents of the inbreaking of God's kingdom into the present world, then in our God-talk we have to ask where God may be found here. In other words, the Body of Christ is called to be involved not just in abstract concepts but in the embodied reality of existence, because this is where God is. Whether at international or at grass-roots level, the Church is bound to be caught up in the redemptive process of justice-making as it seeks, by engaging critically and prophetically with the world, to bring in God's kingdom. The praxis of being the Church as the Body of Christ means overturning cultures that unjustly discriminate against any section of society. This may entail, for instance, questioning economic and political institutions that perpetuate an oppressively unequal distribution of land and wealth, or that prevent reasonable access to the legal system. We have seen the application of these principles, for example, in calls by the worldwide Church for debt relief for developing countries. Many parishes have supported the Make Poverty History initiative launched in 2005. Where we recognize God's presence in any situation, then we need to appropriate the transformative potential of that presence to work for justice and seek to change systems that tolerate injustice.

The imperative of doing justice applies to the Church itself as much as to the secular world. To this end, the Church needs to ensure that its structure, its language and its symbols all promote rather than hamper the full personhood of all people, including women, in God's image. The stand against unjust discriminatory practices has included a challenge to powerful religious taboos practised by the Church against women, for instance with regard to entering holy places and performing ritual and leadership roles. Sometimes – perhaps where women have begun to develop a measure of self-worth – these taboos have provoked proportionately staunch reactions.

At the turn of the twentieth century, women were doing much hard (often unpaid) work in the mission field, in parish visiting and in Sunday Schools. But they were excluded from the newly formed parochial church councils. The deaconess movement and Anglican sisterhoods were well established; but women were not permitted to speak in public worship, even to read the lesson. The idea of a woman being highly educated and gaining any form of independence was for many abhorrent and unbiblical. In 1924 Maude Royden published a book entitled *The Church and Woman* (Redfern 1999:63). In it she challenged the universal subordination of women and pointed to the radical nature of Jesus' teaching and example in relation to women. Royden was a well-educated, powerful speaker and teacher. Yet she was prevented in the Anglican Church from fully exercising these gifts, forbidden by the bishop, for instance, from giving an address in church. Only in the 1960s were Anglican women generally allowed to preach. It was not until 1987 that women were ordained deacons in the Church of England.

It took the greater part of the last century, and much costly effort by far-sighted campaigners, for the priesthood of women finally to be recognized in the Anglican Communion. In 1974 eleven women were ordained irregularly (without the ratification of Church authorities) in the Episcopal Church of the USA. A year later, the Anglican Church of Canada authorized female ordination, and in the 1980s other provinces started to ordain women priests. The first female priests in the Church of England were ordained in Bristol Cathedral on 12 March 1994, seventy years after the publication of Royden's book. The long road to ordination was, for many of the first female ordinands, an agonizing one. Una Kroll, in her *Anatomy of Survival*, tells how, after a long struggle, she was eventually ordained in the Church in Wales (which accepted women a few years after the Church of England). By then she was 'over retirement age, could never take responsibility for a parish and could never know the delight in exercising "a cure of souls" as a shared exercise with a diocesan bishop' (2001:102). And following her priesting she found, as have other women (including myself), that some members of her congregation refused to recognize her ministry.

Female priests in various Protestant denominations now serve across the globe from Japan to Namibia and Brazil. Nearly half of those now training for the Anglican priesthood in England are female. The Church of England, in 2008, voted to allow women bishops. The USA saw the first female bishop, Barbara Harris, in 1989, and in 2006 Katharine Jefferts Schori became the first female Primate in the worldwide Anglican Communion. Since then other provinces have followed – Canada, Polynesia, Cuba, Australia, New Zealand and Sweden. The Church in Ireland and the Scottish Episcopal Church, as well as those in a number of other provinces, have voted for women bishops but have yet to appoint one. Yet the priesthood of women is still by no means universally accepted. Provincial Episcopal Visitors, or 'flying bishops', minister to those parishes opposed to women's ordination. In 2008 the General Assembly of the Church of Wales narrowly voted against a move to allow women bishops. Several African provinces and others world-wide do not allow the ordination of women.

In the Roman Catholic Church priesthood continues to be denied to women, and so the women's struggle for recognition has taken rather different paths. For many in the Roman Catholic tradition, simply trying to include women in the ordained priesthood as it is now exercised would not be the solution to long-held discriminatory practices. Instead, some writers, such as Mary Hines, urge for a radical transformation of the whole church institution to rid it of constraining patriarchal and hierarchical structures (1993:163). Others, whether Roman Catholic or Anglican, argue that it is important for women to be ordained even if they may subsequently question the nature of priesthood and the institution of the Church as it presently stands.

In the Anglican Church and other denominations where women are now ordained, it is possible to gauge how the woman priest contributes to the transformation of human relationships as part of the process of redemption. If redemption involves working to bring in God's kingdom, how then does she symbolize the Church's prophetic call to overcome those oppressive structures and ideologies that prevent the kingdom breaking in? Since discrimination against women has been rampant throughout church history and still thrives today, the priest who is a woman is inevitably a member of a subordinated group. She is also a member of Christ's Body, the Church, which is called to offer a prophetic voice against oppression and to seek to establish justice and mercy. So she has by her gender a prophetic role to play, standing both with the victims of oppression in the concrete world and also for the call to rid the world of oppression in anticipation of the coming kingdom. She is both an embodied sign of redemption and a member of a marginalized group, and so is well placed to signify the redemptive hope for transformation in human relationships. Her position questions those structures and attitudes in the Church and in wider society that are unjustly discriminatory. She therefore represents the outcome not only of abstractly thinking a theology of redemption for all people but of concretely doing such a theology.

The woman priest does not refute oppression directed only against women. Since the priest represents the whole Church, she then stands for all those discriminated against unjustly because of age, race, class or any other distinction. As such, she is a figure of hope and promise to all oppressed groups who find themselves on the wrong side of 'otherness' and who have been excluded in some way by mainstream society or culture. She is a challenge to any reigning ideology that seeks to exclude certain groups through unjust discrimination, whether in the Church or in wider society. In a theology of natality, she shows that traditional ideologies of oppression and subjugation exercised by the powerful over 'others' can be overcome.

Male and female together

Where people live and work together and with others harmoniously and effectively, they are likely to do so in an atmosphere of tolerance, respect and giving. In a good working relationship that is mutually nurturing and effective, members will find ways of collaborating that unite individuals but value their diversity of experience and ways of knowing. Communities that practise this sort of collaboration will be free of relationships that unnecessarily subordinate or dominate, and so they provide a supportive, empowering environment in which all individuals and groups may flourish.

Groups that operate in this way reflect the perichoretic movement of the three persons of the Trinity, and in so doing anticipate the eschatological community and new creation that is our ultimate fulfilment as relational beings. The Church is called to be a communion that functions as an icon of the trinitarian God and that offers an effective working model for the whole of society. Where inclusion and diversity are truly valued, then all members enjoy the freedom to attain self-identity and to relate to one another in a way that allows them to mature to full personhood.

If we apply these working principles to the clergy, we might ask: how can priests working together effectively configure and carry out a life of worship and ministry in community that reflects the perichoresis of the triune God? Where the priesthood comprises both sexes, we must then ask: how can a priesthood of both women and men effectively symbolize and model the perichoresis of the Trinity within an institution that does not fully recognize or embrace sexual difference? The culture of the Church, as with wider society, has not always allowed for all humans to flourish. This has been the case especially for those considered to be non-normative. Among these 'others', women are only now finding their voice amid widely-practised discriminatory and exclusionary attitudes and practices. In the Church, as elsewhere, there remains a level of sexual forgetfulness or ignorance that has yet to be understood and overcome, even by those who support a priesthood of both sexes.

When I was first testing my vocation to priesthood, I was interviewed by a senior clergyman. Pressed to explain why I wanted to be ordained, I tried to explain to him that the reason was partly to do with authority: I wanted to be given the authority to become what I felt God was calling me to be. He seemed rather irritated by my reply, as if this answer did not fit into his idea of what a call to ordination means. In turn, I felt deflated and demeaned by his irritation. It occurred to me as I drove home at the end of a somewhat unsatisfactory meeting that he and I were approaching the notion of authority from different angles. He was in a position of considerable authority and power, highly regarded in his ministry. I was a nobody who was being burdened by a calling to which I needed to respond in faith. How could I obey that calling without the authorization of the Church? It seemed to me at the time that the difficulty between us was caused by our each speaking a different language.

This difficulty came to mind several years later when I read Bishop Penny Jamieson's reflections on sexual difference in her interviews with ordinands (Jamieson, 2004:120–33). She notes the variation in responses in relation to authority, contrasting the confident and dominating style perceived to belong to men with the more diffident and inclusive style of women. Her own experience has taught her that women ordinands often stress a vocation for service rather than seeking power. They feel the need, however, for the authorization which ordination bestows on them. Male prospective ordinands, on the other hand, often do not feel any need to seek authorization in this way, since leadership is expected of them – indeed they expect it of themselves. Men tend to assume authority without difficulty but find it harder than women to move into more mutual and relational roles. Jamieson observes that women and men often approach matters of relationship and authority from different perspectives, and she stresses the need for patterns of mutuality in leadership that will build up the whole Christian community.

The question of authority is just one illustration of how, in all forms of human community, modes of being and of working together are broadly gendered. The Church, as a bastion of male-dominated, hierarchical structures and traditions, has yet to adjust fully to the influx of women who think and function in ways different from their male predecessors and colleagues. Female clergy are still very much a minority group within a male-oriented institution, and clearly recent research on sexual differences in ways of knowing and being in relation have not provoked an overnight sea change in its structures or behaviours. The Freudian dictum that 'women are altogether taboo' still appears to hold ground, at least in some areas of the Church, and may go some way in explaining women's difficulties in colonizing a hitherto all-male territory. There abound well-documented incidents of hostile treatment meted out by men on female clergy. There remains conscious prejudice against women in leadership roles in the Anglican Church, where a 'stained-glass ceiling' bars women from the episcopate in most provinces. Professional development can be problematic even within current boundaries. Organizational structures can work against ordained women by failing to provide clear career patterns that cater for their particular needs and responsibilities. Beyond this, there is an anachronistic attitude that has not caught up with contemporary thinking about women in positions of leadership and authority. (For a collection of arguments for the case, see Harris and Shaw, 2004.)

Full acceptance of clergywomen within the authority structure of the Church as yet remains a long-term aspiration towards a fundamental shift in the values of our culture. It will require a type of paradigm shift that is possible only when sexual difference is recognized, accepted and acted upon by those in authority in the institution of the Church. Come that day, women's ways of knowing and being, although different from those of men, will be understood as equally valuable and valid. In the institutional Church especially, bound as it is to ancient traditions and practices, change in attitudes and behaviours is inevitably slow and incremental, and will be resisted as unwelcome by some members. Institutional practices can be analysed and sometimes changed, but inevitably with difficulty, stress and resistance. And those who resist change can become highly defensive, mistrustful and hostile towards those they feel threaten the status quo, as many ordained women know to their cost.

Once within a male-dominated institution, women have broadly two options in the approach they adopt. They can confront or oppose the institutional culture, in which case they may incur unpopularity and cause themselves great stress. Or they can conform to it in a way that is disjunctive with their own way of being. I found this was a tension for me when I worked as a chaplain in a male prison where female staff were much in the minority. It was a place where patriarchy was taken as the norm, where entrenched prejudices thrived, where sexism and racism, although unacceptable in theory, were rife in practice. I resisted adopting 'masculine' speech or behaviours that would conform with an overwhelmingly male-dominated environment. My characteristically 'feminine' behaviour was sometimes read by male officers as soft or sentimental. I tried to work collaboratively with staff and inmates, but (other than within the chaplaincy and the education department, where the ratio of female staff was higher) I found this difficult in an extremely hierarchical environment characterized by mistrust, noncooperation and confrontational behaviour.

In 2000, Helen Thorne conducted a study of the first women to be ordained as priests in England. She found that, although her respondents mostly preferred a collaborative and facilitative style of ministry, they were 'not particularly egalitarian in their attitude to

Church affairs, nor [were] they concerned to de-emphasise their clerical status' (2000:149). Having been denied positions of authority and leadership for so long, it is hardly surprising that these first women priests should fail to challenge patriarchal traditions in the institution they had just joined. The women were under much pressure to conform to the status quo and prove their success within the existing establishment. No doubt sensitive to their detractors, it was probably enough, even among those who saw the need for transformation, to prove their worth within the institution rather than directly challenge male-dominated church structures and values.

Those who hold power relinquish it with difficulty. Where there are hierarchical, power-dominated structures, then those who believe that a collaborative and gender-inclusive ministry is a theologically sound way of working have an onerous task. They are faced with bringing about a fundamental shift in attitudes and working practices. In a discussion document published by the Church in Wales, Joanna Penberthy, a serving vicar, comments on the ongoing problems for women and men clergy working alongside each other equitably. She notes that the first cohort of women to be ordained there were tired of campaigning and glad simply to get on with ministry. 'Perhaps we did not keep account of what was happening sufficiently rigorously and have not supported the women coming after us as we should have done' (Penberthy, 2006:18).

Meanings for our time and place

It is to the current cohort of clergywomen, those who followed their pioneer colleagues and have largely avoided the bruising struggle for acceptance, that the task of working towards recognition of sexual difference belongs. Ordained women form the catalyst that brings this cultural transformation somewhat closer, not least because female experience and representation of the divine are brought into corporeal presence at the Eucharist. The woman priest may or may not consciously choose to adopt practices such as inclusive language or 'feminine' working styles. But her bodily presence at the altar alone highlights the need for a shift in the prevailing religious culture to acknowledge overlooked or ignored female aspects of the divine and the divine within the feminine. Her presence alone refutes all those negative historic connotations that have hindered a full bodying forth of all the rich and complex meanings that arc between the woman and the divine. She plays a key role in overcoming traditional interpretations of religion according to asymmetrical connotations of gender that overlook or devalue the feminine.

In this way, we are able to reinterpret ancient, polysemic symbols (that is, symbols bearing more than one sense or meaning) so as to 'hear again' meanings that are true and appropriate to our time and place. For example, we know that God is neither male nor female and is portrayed in Scripture in a variety of ways where gender designation is fluid. We might call to mind Jesus using the simile of the hen and chicks in describing his love for the people of Jerusalem (Matt. 23.37); or the portrayal of Wisdom/Sophia in the Book of Proverbs; or other maternal symbols for God, as discussed in Chapter 3. Thinking of God in terms of neutral or female designations as well as male reflects the fluidity of the divine gender shown in Scripture but restricted by a male-only priesthood. Male and female priests together reinforce this constellation of symbolic possibilities for the triune God, and, liberated from the constrictions of an exclusively male way of thinking, space is opened up for exploring a range of metaphors for the divine–human relationship and for forms of human relations. Male and female priests ministering together can help the Church to revision itself beyond rigid, traditional ritual and social roles towards the kind of relationships that better reflect the perichoresis of the triune God.

There is a healing role to play in this opening up of fluid gender symbols associated with the sacred. We have seen how traditional, masculinist metaphors for God have always been dominant in patriarchal societies; and how cultural practices are read back to describe and interpret the nature of God. So in an androcentric culture, God and the sacred are interpreted and symbolized through a male lens. Where God is almost exclusively seen in man's image, there is a danger not only of the feminine being ignored and devalued, but of women being subjected to dehumanizing, abusive treatment. Nuala O'Faolain, in her memoir, tells the sad, familiar story of children, wives and mothers physically abused by men in their homes, but never able to protest, nor given any support by their priest (1999).

Such a failure of justice and mercy – on the part of the abuser and of the Church – is rooted in a hierarchical, patriarchal culture that has forgotten to value and nurture all its people. For the

Church, one way to start overcoming the oppressive, damaging patterns of gender relations is to start with its religious symbols. Where God can be imagined in a range of gendered symbolic configurations, then the divine is no longer dominantly conceived through the masculine. And where God is symbolized not only through the masculine but also through the feminine, then the presumption of asymmetric gender relations, with male dominance and female subservience, is undercut. By this means the male-dominated interpretation of women's sexuality (as we saw with Hosea's treatment of Gomer, see p. 33) is called into question as a social construct.

The damaging notion of a male God and an eternal, divinely prescribed male hegemony has increasingly been challenged and undermined by theologians, social activists and artists. A bronze sculpture created in 1974 by Edwina Sandys was shown in the Cathedral of St John The Divine, New York. Entitled *Christa*, it depicts a crucified female form and caused much controversy when it was first exhibited. Yet it was found to carry restorative power for many female survivors of male violence, because these women saw that it resonated with their own suffering. They found it freed them from the guilt they bore, the burden of imagining that, being female, they deserved their abuse. *No Longer Strangers*, a source book published by the World Council of Churches, includes a picture of a Christa sculpture. With it is an anonymous poem entitled 'By his wounds you have been healed', written by a victim of sexual abuse inspired by this image. It ends:

I will no longer hide these wounds of mine.
I will bear them gracefully.
They tell a resurrection story.
(Gjerding and Kinnamon, 1983:33)

There have since been several artists who have depicted Christ through the female form, causing shock and revulsion from some, while for others (and perhaps especially for women who have little sense of selfhood and self-worth) these images are liberating and empowering. In this context, the woman priest as a symbolic figure (as well as pastorally) may have a particular role in helping survivors of male sexual abuse to relate to a God whose hitherto dominantly male designations have been a barrier to worship and to the spiritual life (Wootton, 2000:93). A male colleague told me that as a child

111

he had suffered abuse from his father, and that his mother had done nothing to intervene. He found in the Eucharist both a challenge and an opportunity for healing:

> I had to come to grips with the fact that I feared the power of God to hurt me, and distrusted the power of God to save me. Having both sexes and both genders represented [in the priesthood] helped me to avoid the mistake of imprisoning the image of God in the image of my parents.

Humankind and the created world: good stewardship

When I and four other deacons were priested, we stood before the bishop barefoot. Not because we had forgotten to wear shoes, but because we felt our barefootedness symbolized for us the calling of priesthood humbly to love and care for all of creation in God's name. That message was further emphasized as we processed outside at the end of the service and, over our stoles, donned streamers bearing the message 'Make Poverty History'. It seemed appropriate that this campaign coincided with a confirmation of our own calling to priesthood.

The Eucharist, as we have seen, is a celebration and feast where the bread of life is shared and which anticipates the heavenly banquet in which all God's people will participate. In celebrating the Eucharist we are spiritually fed and nurtured in order to prepare us for going out to work for God's kingdom. Part of that work is to oppose unjust and discriminatory practices that do not respect either the dignity of all people or the intrinsic value of nature; and the woman priest serves an important symbolic function in this regard. By her gender she is traditionally the dominated, the marginalized, the one close to earth and nature; yet as a priest she represents the divine, the kingdom to which believers aspire, the Church which is the Body and Bride of Christ. In this representative role, and particularly in presiding at the Eucharist, she is a witness against any excluding and discriminatory practices. And through the initiator of the Eucharist, Jesus Christ, she is a potent signifier of the reconnection of day-to-day human life with all of creation.

In the material world, the daily preparation and serving of food has always largely been the domain of women. Yet the tradition of confining the presidency of the Eucharist to a male clerical elite has excluded women, those who generally carry out the main burden of caring and nurturing tasks. So there has been a disjunction between our ordinary lives and the spiritual life, nurtured ritually by men who have served as symbols for all people. We find the same case with other priestly roles. A key notion in baptism is that of giving birth, the priest gives spiritual sustenance to the sick and dying, nurtures and teaches those taking their first steps on the spiritual path, and tries to serve all who ask for spiritual nourishment. There are obvious comparisons to be made here between the priestly calling and the roles of birthing, caring and feeding common to women worldwide. How apt, then, that women should themselves also be represented in the priesthood, where these roles are translated into spiritual attributes.

The presence of female priests remakes the link between spiritual life and day-to-day living, with its struggle (for many) to put food on the table, to satisfy hunger, to stave off poverty, to survive and flourish. The Eucharist becomes reconnected with its transformative purpose. There is an added clarity to the call for change in patterns of relationship that recognize the value both of women and of nature. In representing the feminine qualities of natality – fertility, nurturing, caring – that allow the world and its inhabitants to grow and flourish, the woman priest witnesses to the imperative to respect, care for and nurture the earth. In a particular way that can be true only for women, she represents both the brokenness of the world as it is, and the hope of that restoration and healing of relationship between humanity, creation and God that is the Christian hope.

The priest who is a woman, in destabilizing an old, anachronistic symbolism, questions patriarchal notions not only about God and human identity but about the human relationship with creation. As the feminine has traditionally been associated with bodiliness, with the earth, with nature and with sin, so the female priest affirms the growing sense of the goodness of nature, that all people are part of creation, and that no one, whether female or male, is 'above' nature.

Through history, the identification of the feminine with nature has labelled women as inferior, less godlike, more fallen. However, a spirituality that is concerned with natality and flourishing is aware of the healing strength and wholeness that derives from a restored and rightful relationship with nature. The woman priest corrects the error of a dualistic understanding of dominion of the earth as mastery and domination, and stands for our responsibility of nurturing one another and the natural environment through compassionate stewardship. In this way, through engaging with the broken, concrete world, we become part of that redemption affirmed and signified by the breaking of bread at the altar.

6

New covenant, new confidence –
the story so far

'Drink this, all of you; this is my blood of the New Covenant'

During my time as a prison chaplain, I was chatting one day to an inmate who was reminiscing about his life as a youngster in a rural Roman Catholic community in southern Ireland. He talked about the women who looked after the church building and observed that any woman who was appointed to clean around the sanctuary would, of course, be past child-bearing age.

An uneasy association between women's generative power and holy spaces and objects, as illustrated by this casual remark, has permeated virtually all cultures and eras. Its focus is the assumed pervasive charge of menstrual blood, and the contaminating effect of anything or anyone it touches. Its insidious influence figures in Hebrew Scripture and in the historical teachings of the Church. And it still remains in some circles (for instance among certain Orthodox Christians) as a current argument against the priesting of women. The Anglican tradition has historically not been exempt from fears about the contaminating influence of 'unclean' women, and vestiges of this primitive unease are with us even today. Yet women in the Anglican Church these days not only clean the sanctuary: as priests they perform the rites associated with those who are ordained as ministers of the word and sacraments. I want to consider age-old anxieties around the issue of the feminine in the context of the woman priest and the Eucharist. But first, in preparing the ground, I shall look at the background notions of covenant and sacrifice in Scripture and in the history of Christianity.

Covenant and sacrifice

In the eucharistic rite, as the story of the Last Supper is retold by the priest standing at the altar, the institution narrative moves attention to the wine. The text recalls the words of Jesus who, having given thanks, instructs the disciples to drink from the cup, saying, 'This is my blood of the covenant, which is poured out for many' (Mark 14.24). According to Luke and Paul, Jesus speaks of the cup poured out as 'the new covenant in my blood' (Luke 22.20; 1 Cor. 11.25). The covenant idea that Jesus uses here harks back to the ancient covenant between God and people that forms a leit-motif in the Hebrew Scriptures. The term is always connected with the concept of relationship, such as a marriage or a pledge of friendship or mutual obligation, often entered into by an oath or a shared meal.

In the history of Israel, the covenant embodied the recognition and commitment between Yahweh and his people, and it was crucial in keeping Israel's worship distinct from that of other contemporary religions and cultures. The stories of Noah and Abraham are associated with covenant traditions. So too is that of Moses, Yahweh's chosen instrument to rescue the Israelites from slavery and establish them as a covenant community obedient to his law. This law is summarized in the ten commandments given to Moses on Mount Sinai, and is followed in Scripture by detailed regulations regarding worship, including the central act of sacrifice.

The custom of sacrifice has been widely practised by many cultures across the globe and throughout the history of religion. It was an important feature of Israel's cultic life, and it became a focal part of the elaborate religious ritual in the Second Temple, the only place where sacrifices could be offered, until its destruction in AD 70. Sacrifices included those of certain animals, where blood was central to the rite. Leviticus gives details of how, when and why these rituals should be carried out. There were sacrifices, for example, for purification after childbirth (Lev. 12) and other types of ritual uncleanness. The aim was the maintenance of cultic and moral purity, brought about by the removal of impurities through sacrificial blood.

Expiatory sin-offerings became prominent in the post-Exilic period, when a sense developed of God's judgement on the nation's disobedience. Worshippers saw sin-offerings as a God-given means of wiping away iniquities that prevented the community from fulfilling the obligations of the covenant relationship. A peace offering was made as a sacrifice of thanks and praise, and was followed by the offerer eating what was left of the sacrifice at a common meal with friends, the priests having consumed the breast and shoulder (Lev. 10.14). Unclean creatures such as dogs and pigs, and usually also those with any defect, could not be offered in sacrifice (Lev. 22:20). The central element of the sacrifice was the oblation of blood on the altar by the priest (Lev. 1.5, 3.2, 4.5). The blood was never to be consumed but, since it gave life to the body, was to be offered by the priest as an atonement for the sin committed by the person bringing the offering (Lev. 5.10).

The New Covenant

The concept of atonement is one which has continued from its Jewish ancestry through the life of the Christian Church, carrying with it something of a sense of brokenness and disruption in the relationship with God which was put right by the once-for-all self-offering of Jesus Christ. For the early Christians, a new order had been established through the blood of Jesus, his death, resurrection and ascension – hence the liturgical focus on the Lord's Supper. He is the mediator of the New Covenant that is not of the law, but of grace and truth (John 1.17). He is welcomed by John the Baptist as Bridegroom to the Church (John 3.29), the one who mediates the New Covenant that promises an eternal inheritance. This New Covenant no longer relates to particular, binding contracts which fallen humans can never fully keep, but is renewable, through the grace given at the Eucharist, in full acceptance of human sinfulness and God's forgiveness.

The first Christians acknowledged Christ's death as the supreme sacrifice, and animal sacrifice, associated with the Old Covenant, was now unnecessary. The early Church came into being within the boundaries of the Roman Empire whose citizens worshipped and sacrificed to a large pantheon of gods and goddesses. In the context of this culture, where religion without sacrifice was inconceivable, the refusal of Christ's followers to offer material sacrifices led to their being thought of as atheists. However, despite this refusal, the religious language and ritual of the early Church remained rich in sacrificial imagery. Paul writes: 'our paschal lamb, Christ, has been sacrificed' (1 Cor. 5.7) and he speaks of Christ as one who 'gave himself up for us, as fragrant offering and sacrifice to God' (Eph. 5.2). The Epistle to the Hebrews expresses the notion that the whole sacrificial law of the Old Testament is fulfilled and superseded by the sacrifice of Christ. The author, referring to Christ removing sin by sacrificing himself, reflects the traditional belief in the expiatory nature of blood sacrifice, for 'without the shedding of blood there is no forgiveness of sins' (Heb. 9.22). The once-for-all nature of Christ's atoning act is here contrasted with that of the Jewish high priest which required constant repetition. Through Christ's death the New Covenant was made, and the sins of the faithful who enter into this new relationship will not be remembered (Heb. 8.12). The notion of a day of judgement of sins, and the traditional Day of Atonement, when the priest would make atonement for all the people (Lev. 16.33), were brought to fulfilment in and through the death of Christ. His sacrificial death enabled liberation from evil and restoration of humankind's relationship with the divine.

The renewal of Christ's New Covenant of grace became focused in the Eucharist, the central rite of memorial, remembrance, covenant, sacrifice and transformation. Followers now regarded worship as offering not material but spiritual sacrifices: the earliest understanding of the offertory in the Eucharist was as a sacrifice of thanksgiving.

The question as to whether this rite is actually a sacrifice has since been a matter of heated debate, culminating in the Reformation. Arguments raged between Reformers and papalists in the sixteenth century about the precise nature of the sacrifice of the mass. Protestants argued among themselves about many issues of belief, but were united in denying that the Eucharist was an actual sacrifice. In the Reformed Church any sacerdotal implications and expressions relating to sacrifice were expunged from the liturgy for the ordering of priests and from the communion service. In the Thirty-Nine Articles, finalized in 1571 as the defining statements of Anglican doctrine, Article 31 repudiates the 'sacrifices of Masses' as 'blasphemous fables, and dangerous deceits'.

The issue of the sacramental presence of the sacrifice of Christ in the Eucharist remains one of debate among Anglicans, between the Roman Catholic and Anglican Churches, and among other denominations. The Eucharist is seen variously as a sacrifice, although not separate or additional to that of Christ on the cross (the view of the Roman Catholic, Eastern Orthodox and High Anglican Churches); and as a holy memorial meal, Christ's sacrifice on the cross having done away with any further need for sacrifice (the view of many Protestants, whose emphasis is on the Eucharist as a sacrifice of worship, praise, thanksgiving and self-offering). Both positions can embrace the notion of individual and communal sacrificial response in terms of joyful self-giving in worship and mission.

The recent process of revision by many denominations of the eucharistic rite has made clear how much Christians now share in common. The Roman Catholic Church has recovered a sense of thanksgiving and memorial as well as sacrifice, while Protestants have found value in the early use of the notion of sacrifice in terms of the memorial of the passion and the continuing work of the cross. Renewed interest in the Jewish origins of the rite has illuminated thanksgiving and supplication as the fundamental features of the Eucharistic Prayer: thanks for the events and truths of the Christian faith, and intercession for the well-being and work of the Church now.

Debate remains as to the precise nature of atonement and the meaning and relevance of sacrifice in relation to the Eucharist. Such debate demonstrates what cannot be contested: that language and imagery of the idea of sacrifice, including the shedding of blood, have always been part and parcel of the Christian narrative, particularly in relation to atonement. Even in low-church Anglicanism, the notion of sacrifice is present in the narrative of the crucifixion and in the offering of worship and service. Sacrifice, albeit subject to various interpretations by the Church, is ingrained within the religious culture of our Christian heritage.

Men, women and blood

The ancient connection between life, blood and sacrifice, intrinsic to the religion of Israel, may now be largely lost to the postmodern imagination. However, blood – so long associated with the symbolism of sacrifice – still carries a powerful charge. In the Christian narrative (as well as in that of other religions) sacrifice and the accompanying shedding of blood is largely related to the masculine imagination and practices carried out by men. The Old Testament tells of blood sacrifices performed by men such as Abraham, Moses and Elijah, usually using male animals (e.g., Gen. 22.13; Exod. 12.5; 1 Kings 18.23). Christ the male saviour sheds his blood for our salvation. Those who consecrate the elements at the altar are overwhelmingly (in some denominations exclusively) men. In secular stories, too, we more often hear of male blood being shed than of women's and it is usually through particularly masculine activities such as fighting and war. We can see this, for example, in the tragic accounts of young soldiers immortalized by the poet Wilfred Owen:

> Happy are men who yet before they are killed
> Can let their veins run cold.
>
> (Allott, 1962:120)

When men bleed, it is usually associated with a wounding through combat, an accident, an assault, a self-sacrifice. The knight slays the evil dragon; the priest of ancient times offers a sacrifice for a battle won; young lads (at least before HIV/AIDS) seal their brotherhood with their own blood; folk leaders fight for their people's freedom (the Mayan hero of Mel Gibson's film *Apocalypto*, who overcomes seemingly insurmountable obstacles to save his wife and child, or the dashing soldier and lover of Louis de Bernieres' novel *Captain Corelli's Mandolin*, on the 'wrong' side yet representative of decency and gallantry). There is often a link between men's blood and heroism or bravery that is not so often made with women. Indeed, exceptions to this only reinforce the general rule. For instance, news bulletins announced the death in May 2006 and June 2008 of the first British female soldier serving in Iraq and Afghanistan respectively. The news caused widespread comment in the media and reignited debate about the propriety of women serving on the front line in areas of conflict.

It is usually the case that, for a man, the sight of his own blood is associated in some way with violence or trauma. In normal, everyday life, men do not come into contact with their own or another's blood. When they do, it usually accompanies heightened emotion or awareness: the shock of injury, the awe of the eucharistic sacrifice, the exhilaration of the sports field, the fear and excitement of watching childbirth.

Women's experience of blood is generally rather different. Female blood is intimately connected with the daily round, the monthly cycle, rhythms of birth and death, fecundity, fertility, labour and rest, emotional changes, periods of engagement or withdrawal. The onset of blood can trigger celebration, hope, relief, despair. Blood is central to the healthy life of normally functioning young women. Blood signals the beginning of adulthood, the pleasure or disappointment of the empty womb; its cessation indicates the start of another's life or the ending of one chapter and the beginning of a new phase. Given the importance of blood in the lives of women, and their intimate connection with natural bloodshed, it seems reasonable to ask why, throughout Judaeo-Christian history (and that of other cultures), religious rites associated with blood have been performed almost exclusively by men.

Not only have women been barred from blood sacrifice, it is also the case that their own natural bloodshedding has hardly figured in the discourses of society – the arts, literature and so on. The one exception seems to be when women's blood is treated as a medical 'problem', investigated by gynaecologists and addressed occasionally by women's magazines and (in recent years) alternative comedians. When women's blood has been portrayed in art and literature, it has invariably been in association with violence done to them, often in the form of murder or rape or another form of sexual abuse. The Hebrew Scriptures feature a number of such instances, including Lot offering his daughters to the men of Sodom for their sexual satisfaction (Gen. 19); the rape of Dinah (Gen. 34:2); the rape and murder of the Levite's concubine (Judg. 19); and Jephthah, following a rash oath, having to sacrifice his daughter (Judg. 11).

In the secular arena, author Michael Frayn, in his novel *Headlong*, predicts that a moderate collection of classical fine art today would probably contain 'Lucretia being raped by Tarquin, and Europa by the bull; Prosperine being carried off by Pluto, and the Sabine women by the Romans; various gang rapes of nymphs by assorted gods and centaurs; and a number of last-minute rescues' (1999:100).

Resistance to sexual abuse figures large in the realm of female Christian saints. They are often remembered because of their vulnerability as virgins to rape, forced marriage and other forms of violence perpetrated upon them. The story of St Winifred, for example, is of a seventh-century Welsh girl who is the victim of attempted rape by a prince. As she flees towards a church, the prince catches her and cuts off her head. A monk replaces Winifred's head, prays over her and she is restored to life. She becomes a nun and eventually abbess at Gwytherin. Where her head fell, at Holywell, legend says that a spring of healing water broke forth. The well has ever since been a place of pilgrimage and healing, and remains today open to visitors.

A much more recent example is that of Manche Masemola, born in the Transvaal just before the First World War. Her family were of the Pedi tribe, most of whom still practised their traditional tribal religion. She began to attend Christian classes offered by missionaries, and her parents, fearful that she might refuse to marry, tried to discourage her with beatings. They finally killed her. Manche's burial place became a site of pilgrimage, and in 1975 her name was added to the calendar of the Province of South Africa. A statue of her now stands with those of nine other twentieth-century martyrs from across the world on the west front of Westminster Abbey.

Purity and defilement

When I was eight years old, my mother, who had caught a cold and was confined to the house, asked me to run an errand to the local shop. Instead of saying what she wanted, she gave me a sealed envelope to hand to the shopkeeper. When I was older I realized that what she had required were sanitary towels. At the time, as I skipped off along the road, I was simply aware that whatever I was fetching for her was something mysterious and secret, whose name must not be spoken. Generations of girls (and boys) have been taught to associate the menses not only with mystery and secrecy but also with shame. Menstrual blood evokes shame in a way that does not pertain to any other form of bloodshedding, male or female.

The distinct difference in treatment between the bloodshed of men and that of women can be interpreted from the viewpoint of purity systems that evolved over long periods of time in order to safeguard a community from defilement. Avoidance of defilement is a recurring theme in religion and our reaction to feelings of fault and our rites of purification are intimately connected to a dread of the impure. Since purity systems often relate to bodily orifices, their regulations usually concern food, waste products, bloodshed (including menstruation), sexual emissions, sexual acts, birth and death. Purity as the avoidance of dirt is a strong theme in the biblical treatment of morality; and in the ethic of purity, dirtiness is wrong and must be avoided, put right or punished.

In Jewish culture and elsewhere, taboos, laws and customs evolved over several centuries as Yahweh's people, through the mediation of the priests, sought to follow the sovereign will of God. We can discern the association of cleanness with obedience to God's will, for instance, when Ezekiel prophesies that there will be a new covenant between God and his people: 'you shall be clean from all your uncleannesses' (Ezek. 36.25). The concern to safeguard a consecrated community, founded on justice and holiness, and to separate it from the defilements of the surrounding pagan world, is reflected in customs and taboos pertaining to personal hygiene and health. The term 'taboo' derives from a notion developed in Polynesian societies of things or places that are too sacred to be spoken of or interfered with. Taboo things are forbidden because of the danger inherent in contact with them. Taboos around childbirth and menstruation signify something sacred (with generative, life-giving power) but also unpredictable and mysterious (with good and/or bad associations, which must be kept in check) and to be avoided and kept apart (the dirty and polluting). Many communities worldwide developed a range of taboos and practices that fell somewhere along this continuum.

Israel evolved a highly structured purity system, aimed at avoiding sin by regulating definitions of 'clean' and 'dirty', and staying clear of anything or anyone considered to be contaminating. The fear of defilement infused its many instructions concerning purity. Paul Ricoeur underlines the link in Israel's history between defilement and sin, commenting that, even with increasing influences between Greek and other cultures, 'the Greeks never attained the feeling of sin in its peculiar quality and with the intensity of which only the people of Israel supply an example' (1967:34). In this patriarchal society, where maleness was normative, cultural purity systems defining cleanness and dirtiness tended to regard men as more closely reflecting and representing the divine, while women were seen as less complete, less holy. This belief was reflected also in women's subordinate legal status and their general exclusion from certain cultic and religious practices, regardless of issues of uncleanness. In the Jewish community marriage and property laws much favoured men:

polygamy was tolerated; women could rarely secure divorce. Women were excluded from Temple duties because of their 'uncleanness' (Lev. 15). At the Temple, they were confined to their own court, the closest they could get to the sanctuary, and only then when not ritually impure. A religious leader became defiled simply by looking on a woman.

Women's blood was of particular concern. Childbirth, for example, was subject to purity codes. Leviticus 12 gives regulations for a woman's post-partum uncleanness. For a son, the mother remains unclean for seven days, the same period as for menstruation. Then, following the boy's circumcision, she must wait thirty-three days to be purified from her bleeding, during which time she must not touch or approach anything holy. For a daughter, the period is two weeks and sixty-six days respectively, reflecting, perhaps, the cultic inferiority of the female sex. Leviticus 15 gives regulations for discharges causing uncleanness, including the menses (Lev. 15.19–30). Levitical rules indicate that not only is the menstruant ritually unclean, but that anyone who comes into contact with her, including her husband, is also unclean. Sexual intercourse is banned at this time as an unlawful sexual relation, alongside bestiality and incest (Lev. 18.19). The punishment for transgressors of this regulation is to be 'cut off from their people' (Lev. 20.18). Return to normal life after the menses follows the sacrifice of a sin offering and a burnt offering. Any flow of blood outside the usual period of menstruation also marks a woman as unclean; her natural bloodshed puts her into a state of ritual defilement. Vaginal bleeding prevents women (along with, for instance, lepers and ejaculants) from entering the sacred precinct of the Temple.

In the Jewish purity system, laws pertaining to the menstruating woman were called *hilkhot niddah*, the latter word connoting abhorrence and repulsion. Ezekiel's description of Israel's conduct as a nation compares it to 'the uncleanness of a woman in her menstrual period in [God's] sight' (Ezek. 36.17). Scholarly discussions often responded to menstruation with fear and disgust, and linked it with a general pernicious influence by the menstruant on the environment: turning wine to vinegar, for instance, or begetting degenerate children. Even her breath and speech cause impurity in others.

Jewish scholar Jonah Steinberg observes that rabbis through late antiquity and medieval times invoked notions of danger and disgust to urge compliance of the *hilkhot niddah*. Men were encouraged to respond with fear and revulsion to the menstruating woman (1997:8). He argues that by attributing to the menstruant a physically and spiritually corrupting odium, and by normalising and privileging a reaction of disgust, an impact is made on perceived and experienced female identity and gender relations 'along the ritualized and mythologized boundary of sex' (1997:24). The regulations of *hilkhot niddah* developed within an interpretive context typified by an assumption of an 'unwholesome, even corrupt or pernicious nature inherent in menstruation and, by extension, in womanhood itself' (1997:25).

A more positive Orthodox view is given by Blu Greenberg, who defends the practice as generating 'a different sense of self for a woman, a feeling of autonomy', building character as a Jewish woman and restoring an 'element of holiness to our bodies, our selves' (2003:242). However, an attitude of suspicion and distaste has remained constant. An assumed unwholesomeness is evident, for instance, in Job. Referring to a mortal born of woman, he asks: 'Who can bring a clean thing out of an unclean?' (Job 14.4). The implication is that the womb is an unclean place whose menstrual and human issue must be subject to the regulations of a purity system. The notion of the generally defiling effect of women occurs in Exodus 19.10–15 where, to achieve an adequate consecration at Mount Sinai, those listening to Moses are told not to go near a woman.

William Countryman, in his study of sexuality in the context of biblical purity codes and property rights, suggests that in the Torah, 'women appear to be a more virulent source of the contagion of impurity than men' (1998:29). He argues that texts concerning harlots and divorced, defiled or foreign women (e.g., Lev. 21.7, 14; Deut. 24.1–4) indicate a wide-ranging anxiety about the polluting potential of women, especially during menstruation and around childbirth. The 'normal' state of a woman, Countryman suggests, is non-menstrual, especially where the ideal woman 'married at puberty and, from then on, remained more or less continually either pregnant or nursing until menopause' (1998:26). A modern woman's natural bodily functions, according to the strict purity codes of Judaism, would put her in a ritually unclean and impure state for about 150 days every year from puberty to menopause.

Women today would by this measure be defined as 'abnormal' for about 40 per cent of their biologically productive lives.

Women's bloodshed: the sacred and the taboo

The constraints and restrictions applied by Jewish and other purity systems to women's bloodshed have been attributed by many writers to a deep-seated fear of female powers evident and ingrained in virtually every patriarchal culture. Researchers from various disciplines have, over the last generation, analysed this phenomenon, and many would agree that women's blood is a sign of the generative power which women have always possessed and which men have always feared.

Efforts to keep society 'clean and proper' led to measures to control and restrict the power of females, particularly fertile women, and contact between the sexes. The Roman naturalist Pliny the Elder, for example, in his *Historia Naturalis*, reports on the virulent effects of the menstrual flow. Irremediable evils result from menstruation coinciding with an eclipse of the moon or the sun; moreover, the touch of a woman is said to ruin vines, ivy and rue. These were the views current in the Roman world at the time of Jesus of Nazareth. I have already noted the radical and countercultural inclusiveness of the Jesus community, and the many women who played key roles in witness and mission. This community of equals provided a model for challenging and transforming contemporary hierarchical structures of society, and included a level of inclusivity towards women that was shocking even to those close to him. His challenge to traditional purity codes included those relating to corpses, to disease and to women.

The story of the haemorrhaging woman illustrates his affirmation of women excluded by society for reasons of ritual impurity (Matt. 9.18–22; Mark 5.21–34; and Luke 8.40–48). It is a story which has historically received little attention as a starting point for exploring the symbolism in the New Testament of defiling female blood. According to Mark, the woman has spent a fortune on consultations with doctors, all to no avail. In all three accounts she approaches Jesus from behind, so that he does not see her. Mark's version explains that she has heard about Jesus; both Matthew and Mark have her reasoning that, if she can only touch Jesus' cloak, she believes she will be healed. Immediately she does this, according to Luke, her haemorrhaging stops and, Mark adds, she knows herself to be cured. Jesus turns round, aware, as Mark and Matthew put it, that power has gone out from him. He asks the crowd who has touched his clothes, and in Mark and Luke his disciples wonder how he can pose such a question when the crowd is crushing around them. But Jesus persists, and the woman comes forward, according to Mark and Matthew in great trepidation. Having listened to her explanation, and addressing her as daughter, Jesus tells her that her faith has healed her, and to go in peace. It is at this moment, according to Matthew, that she recovers.

There has been some discussion about whether the woman in this story was actually suffering from chronic vaginal bleeding, and therefore whether her encounter with Jesus can be read in the light of Leviticus 15 and the taboos associated with menstruants (see, for instance, Jackson, 1998:85). However, it might be argued that she comes to Jesus in 'fear and trembling' (as described by Mark and Luke), not because of her illness but because she is afraid of the wrath of those around her in breaking purity codes (especially in the presence of Jairus, leader of the synagogue), and because she is awed by the presence of a great healer. If this is the case, she would be especially fearful of rendering a respected healer ritually unclean. Yet the woman has faith that Jesus carries greater power than does the contaminating potential of her body's impurity. As both a woman and as a menstruant, she has been debarred from many religious customs and practices, especially those associated with holy objects and sacrifice. The woman, aware that she is breaking strict purity codes by appearing in public and touching Jesus (thus causing him also to be ritually unclean), nevertheless seeks healing from him and tells him her story.

Jesus' response – calling her 'daughter' – upholds her faith and trust in him, and vindicates her actions as praiseworthy rather than socially improper. He makes no mention in this case of any past sin, and his engagement with her goes far beyond a simple act of charity or pity. By simply talking with her – perhaps especially in the presence of Jairus – Jesus signals the overturn of these religious constraints in an inclusive invitation to all to approach the holy, including those regarded as disabled or in some way 'other'. Jesus' public dialogue with her stresses that he is bringing her back into the society that has rejected her. He gives her back her self-respect and spiritual and mental peace as well as a simple cure.

His final command to go in peace uses the Hebrew word *Shalom*, a term which carries a sense of wholeness and soundness. These are qualities that also feature in the story which starts just before the haemorrhaging woman and concludes just after. Here Jesus restores Jairus' twelve-year-old daughter to life and hence to potential fertility in her future womanly life. The two linked stories resonate with elements of death and defilement leading to fecundity and new life. The author of these two overlapping stories shows that the new creation is being ushered in by Jesus who has power over illness, infertility and death. With the restoration of peace and wholeness, the woman experiences through Jesus more than an absence of physical affliction; it is also acceptance, respect and restoration of self-esteem and dignity. Jesus transforms her from the impure, shamed outsider to the accepted, healed and embraced member of the new community of love. He restores women's dignity and value and dismisses any bar to inclusion due to nature and physiology. The message is that women are not to be denied access to the holy simply as a consequence of physiological function.

Menstruation and misogyny

We have seen, however, that within a comparatively short time the radically inclusive nature of Christ's ministry and teaching regarding women had been largely subsumed in the Church's reversion to a patriarchal world-view. His affirmation of the full personhood, status and potential of women in God's image remained largely ignored, disputed or denied through the greater part of church history. Since its inception the Church has been preoccupied with deeply rooted notions about the evil of sexuality, and with fear of the pernicious influence of the feminine and women's generative power. Menstruation continued to evoke widespread hatred. There is arguably a strong connection between these fears and preoccupations and the many gender inequalities which continue to pertain throughout the Church today.

Despite Jesus' teachings, taboos around menstruation were re-established in at least some sections of the early Church. At this time, the mechanism by which Jesus Christ took on human form was a matter of considerable interest. Writers reflected on the maternal body, including the uterus, which was celebrated as the vehicle for life and for God's immanence and incarnation. The womb, the earliest home of each human being, was a source of reverence as a centre for God's creative activity. But it was also a source of sin, and cursed as the source of sexual temptation. Tertullian, for instance, celebrated Jesus' human birth, but still taught that the womb is unclean and disparaged women as the fallen Eve. He famously remarked that women are 'the Devil's gateway . . . the first deserter of the divine law . . . You destroyed so easily God's image, man' (1869:304). Tertullian is here referring to the symbolic association between women in general and Eve, the first woman in the biblical account of creation. Eve was the first to sin: it was she who first took the forbidden fruit. She thereby became subordinate to Adam (Gen. 3.16), and her sin served to justify women's historical inferiority.

The third-century treatise *Didascalia* instructed that women were not unclean during their period and did not need ritual ablutions, a teaching reaffirmed by Pope Gregory I in 601. The fact that an author needed to record such teaching indicates that some were promulgating opposite views. There was certainly discussion at this time as to whether menstruating women should receive Holy Communion. Bishop Dionysius of Alexandria, for instance, forbade women to enter church during their period.

Concomitant with the male abhorrence of menstruation was an increasing restriction on women's liberty, authority and leadership roles, and a lowering of their religious status. By the end of the fourth century, there was already a diminishment in the freedom and opportunity that may well have characterized the first years of the Church. The Council of Laodicea (363) barred women from entering the altar area. Successive councils, popes and synods, on the grounds of women's defiling nature, banned females from the sanctuary, from serving at the altar, from distributing communion, from touching sacred objects and vestments and from entering sacred (male) space. In various dioceses menstruating women were banned from receiving communion and baptism (Bishop Timothy of Alexandria, 680) and from visiting a church (Bishop Theodore of Canterbury, 820). Women who had given birth required reconciliation with the Church (Synod of Treves, 1227), and those who had died in childbirth unreconciled could be denied burial in the churchyard, or might receive a secret burial. Following Pliny, menstruants throughout the medieval period were thought to cause bees to die, milk to sour, metal to rust and men, through intercourse, to become impotent and unsuccessful in war.

The tenth-century Abbot Odo of Cluny taught that to embrace a woman was to embrace a sack of manure. Men in orders were discouraged from associating with women. Purification after childbirth became the norm. Durham Cathedral (founded in 1093) features a Lady Chapel, unusually so named since it was once the only part of the cathedral that could be entered by women according to the rules of the Benedictine order of monks. A little way inside the main cathedral building is a black line in the floor which marked the point beyond which women were not allowed to pass.

The result of this weight of male suspicion and loathing was that women came to view themselves as incapacitated and polluted because of their issue of blood. A misogynistic tendency continued to permeate the medieval clerical establishment. Thomas Aquinas, 132writing in the thirteenth century and influenced by Aristotle, argues in his *Summa Theologica* against women taking holy orders on the grounds that they are, by their nature, incapable of the headship that is exclusive to males. It is a woman's biological body that makes her defective; she is the result of misadventure, something 'defective and misbegotten'. He forbids intercourse with a menstruating woman as a mortal sin because of its detrimental effect on children. The idea that intercourse during menstruation is sinful persisted until relatively recent years, and represents one of a raft of attitudes springing from fear of women's natural powers and physical functions. This fear culminated in the great persecution of so-called witches in western Europe from the fifteenth to seventeenth centuries.

Witches were said to have special powers that could cause fruit trees to blight, crops to wither, storms to gather, cows to dry up and mares to miscarry. Many so-called witches – often women who exercised such crafts as midwifery, herbalism, hypnotism and dowsing – were brought to trial all over Europe. There is uncertainty about the numbers killed: various sources suggest anywhere between 30,000 to 9 million. Although a number of feminist writers have drawn on the phenomenon of the witch hunts, there has until recently been a lack of scholarly research into the historical events, and hence difficulty in the interpretation of historical data. It seems, however, that many more women than men were persecuted, perhaps partly because, in a patriarchal environment, women living alone were socially weak and legally powerless, and so offered an easy target as scapegoats for those misfortunes such as miscarriage and other common threats to a community.

The *Malleus Maleficarum* (*Hammer of Witches*), published in 1484 as a manual for inquisitors, stated that witchcraft derives from carnal lust, which in women is insatiable, and often involves deviant sexual behaviour and diabolical, orgiastic activities directed by Satan to threaten Christian society. It sold more copies, in both Protestant and Catholic regions, than any book except the Bible. The assumed sexual lust of women provided grounds for accusations of witchcraft. Several hundred women met their death in the seventeenth century at the hands of Matthew Hopkins, 'witchfinder general'. Their supposed crime was to have had sexual intercourse with the devil. Methods for executing witches always avoided spilling blood, the source of their power. The caution against the power of women's blood underlines the sexual fear at work in the Church, and the deep physiological roots from which springs the misogyny that underlies the association of women with witchcraft. In male-dominated religion, where the feminine holds a place of powerful ambivalence, the witch figure is the shadow side of the pure virgin and kindly mother symbolized by the Virgin Mary.

The witch hunt did not end with the Reformation. Protestantism emphasized masculine values of order and control, including subjugation of female sexuality, and sought to rid itself of much of the rich maternal symbolism that had flourished in the Middle Ages. In a culture that treated the male sex as closer to the image of God, the female body was seen generally in functional terms, restricted mainly to marriage and procreation. The Virgin Mary, along with other saints, largely disappeared from worship; shrines and places of pilgrimage – including those of importance to women – were desecrated. The symbolic female body, represented predominantly by the Virgin Mary, vanished from view in the years following the Reformation, and at the same time the witch-craze reached its climax. Executions continued in England until 1684 and in Scotland until 1727.

The Protestant reformers continued to assume that menstrual women were subject to sexual and moral defilement. Only ultimate salvation in heaven would transcend the ordinances of creation and punishment linking women with original sin and lust. In the sixteenth century, Martin Luther taught male dominance and extolled obedience to men, marriage and motherhood as the proper role for women. The causal link he made between women, dirt and inferiority is clear in his teaching that women have 'lots of filth and little wisdom' (Wiesner, 1990:123).

The following century saw the birth of the Society of Friends, whose beliefs and practices, in contrast to much of contemporary society, included women's spiritual equality with men. Quakers viewed marriage as an equal partnership and promoted girls' education. From the beginning of the movement in the 1650s, Quaker women preached, published tracts and became missionaries. Within the rest of the Church and in society as a whole, however, women were largely kept from education, decision-making and leadership roles on the grounds of their innate lowly status. The education and training of women for their presumed role in life was a matter of debate in the eighteenth century, and a number of books appeared discussing the nature of the ideal woman. Mary Wollstonecraft's *The Vindication of the Rights of Woman* (1792) offered a passionate argument for women to take their place as productive members of society, rather than be forced into passivity and vanity by the need to please others. Her argument centred largely on the wisdom of parents in educating their daughters sufficiently to become more than the decorative servants of men:

> Strengthen the female mind by enlarging it, and there will be an end to blind obedience; but, as blind obedience is ever sought for by power, tyrants and sensualists are in the right when they endeavour to keep women in the dark, because the former only want slaves and the latter a plaything. (1996:11)

Wollstonecraft's plea came in the context of a prevailing culture of considerable diversity of practices and beliefs relating to women, yet on the whole the belief still held that women's bodily functions rendered them unfit for education and leadership. Women were assumed to be prone to irrationality and derangement, lacking resistance to evil because they were more 'natural' and therefore non-rational. By contrast, men's minds were considered rational and able to govern and direct their physical bodies. Since menstruation was assumed to require a lot of energy, any exercise of intellectual judgement was thought to lead to degeneration of reproductive power, and so intellectual exercise in women was thought to be unfeminine and to lead to sterility.

In the nineteenth century medical experts opined that education also caused hysteria, a term derived from the Greek word for womb and often associated with a disturbance of moral and intellectual faculties. They regarded hysteria as a female condition that could sometimes be 'cured' by clitoral excision. Allowing women more rights might, according to some Victorian teaching, make them ill. Suicide and murder committed by women were thought to be hysterical symptoms of menstrual psychoses. At the turn of the twentieth century, Freud, writing on beliefs about menstruation, pregnancy and childbirth, commented: 'it might almost be said that women are altogether taboo' (*The Collected Papers* 8:75, quoted in Farley, 1990:244). A connection between women and impurity was widespread even in relatively recent times. Scout, the narrative voice in Harper Lee's *To Kill a Mocking Bird*, recalls being taken by the family housekeeper to the local black church, where the pastor's sermon cautioned against 'heady brews, gambling and strange women', the latter considered worse than bootleggers. She often heard such warnings in her own church: 'I was confronted with the Impurity of Women doctrine that seemed to preoccupy all clergymen' (1960:125). Notions of mystery, fear and disgust around the menses persist even today; taboos, ignorance and assumptions of uncleanness are not confined to the past. The idea of menstrual impurity remains strong in many cultures, including that of the Church. Science writer Natalie Angier has shown that even today, the vagina is regarded in many societies and by many people – even medical practitioners in 'developed' countries – as 'dirty' (1999:52). Penelope Shuttle and Peter Redgrove, with the intention of arguing that menstruation is not Eve's curse but rather women's friend, searched for literature relating to the psychology of menstruation and found that, until the mid-1970s, no such literature existed. The subject of menstruation was evidently still taboo, kept under a veil of suspicion and ignorance. The womb, and by association all women, have tended to be associated in male-dominated culture not only with procreation but also with evil and sin. Consequently, women are subject to a degree of apprehension and suspicion. Luce Irigaray argues that many men fantasize about the womb not as a place where we become body but as 'a devouring mouth ... a sewer in which anal and urethral waste is poured ... a threat to the phallus' (1993:16). Feelings of fear and anxiety aroused by the uterus (and the maternal body in general) are evident today in the way the female body is co-opted in language. One of the most insulting swearwords in the English language refers to the place where human life is first conceived. Overall, the womb has been prey to suspicion, fear, anxiety and ignorance, if not downright misogyny.

Fear and shame

Whether denied, veiled or ignored, fear undoubtedly lingers. Patriarchy continues largely to define women in terms of their relationship to men. As Eve is the dangerous temptress and Mary of Nazareth the saint, so women have been polarized and portrayed starkly as either (bad) whores or (good) virgins, in the gutter or on a pedestal. Either way, women's identity and therefore their capacity to image the divine is closely tied to, and devalued because of, their bodiliness. Men's ambivalent attitude to women, their bodies, their bodily functions and their sexuality is related to a fragmented and distorted view of sexuality and its purported association with impurity and evil. The paradox of men's simultaneous desire, fear and abhorrence of women's bodies is summed up by a male character in *On the Contrary*, a novel by André Brink:

> What is this shameful reasoning? Because you are a maid you must be a whore. Because you are a woman you must be a whore. Because I can defile you you must be a whore. Because I despise myself you must be a whore. Because I am a man you must be a whore.
>
> (Brink, 2000:174)

Brink here cogently illustrates the tendency in patriarchal culture to put one half of humanity at odds with the other and so to create unequal and oppressive relationships. But do we have to read the stories of the Fall and of the eviction from Eden as a depiction of women's peculiar proneness to evil or of their secondary status? These are assumptions that inevitably open the way for the sort of dehumanizing aggression expressed by Brink's character. Another reading would be that the story tells of the age-old incomplete and dysfunctional relationship between the sexes, lived out in a patriarchal culture in which women are perceived as 'other', inferior and associated with evil. Following this line of thought, woman's subordination to man is a result not of the order of creation but of the Fall, and reflects the sinful disordering of relationships as a consequence of human rebellion against God. Part of such a rebellion is the human appetite for domination and power. This causes people to deny their interdependency with one another, and leads to exploitation of subordinates and of the earth.

That which is feared (according to the logic of patriarchy) must be overcome, ordered and controlled so that it poses less of a threat. That this deep-seated fear and the taboos it engenders are finally being addressed may be evidenced by the enormous success of Eva Ensler's play *The Vagina Monologues*, which has been performed in dozens of languages and countries since its first run in 1996. It features a series of monologues all related to the vagina, for instance through menstruation, rape, orgasm and childbirth. A recurring theme is the vagina as an instrument of female empowerment and the embodiment of female individuality. Having seen a production at a theatre in Glasgow packed with a female audience set on enjoying a good Saturday night out, I can personally testify to the play's empowering and liberating effect on women.

Recent feminist research has similarly sought to rehabilitate menstruation from connotations of shame and fear. Spiritual feminism, for instance, seeks to revive what its advocates see as the sacred nature of menstruation: its ambiguous, powerful charge, they argue, is exactly what makes it sacred and so eligible for high religious status. It is arguable that in sacralizing menstrual power, as in spiritual feminism, there is a healing effect that helps to overcome the tradition of otherness and exclusion caused not so much because women are profane, as because patriarchy senses that they are too sacred. Both patriarchy's abhorrence and spiritual feminism's celebration of menstruation acknowledge that women's blood has a powerful 'charge' because it approaches something of the divine source of life and death.

Women and self-sacrifice

We have seen that an understanding of the concept of sacrifice in relation to blood must include an analysis of sexual difference, since women's blood (and hence women themselves) has always been treated differently from that of men. I now want to look at another sort of sacrifice that is integral to the Christian tradition, that of self-sacrifice, which again requires a gendered analysis.

In response to Christ's giving of his body and blood for our new life, we offer at the Eucharist, in the words of Prayer A, our 'sacrifice of thanks and praise' whereby we give ourselves in anticipation of the coming kingdom, to bring life and redemption to a broken world. Christ's once-for-all offering of himself for humankind evokes a response of self-giving in members of his Body on earth, 'offering ourselves as a reasonable, holy and living sacrifice' (Rom. 12.1). The notion of sacrifice here, then, applies to ourselves, to our self-surrender to the mercy and sovereign will of God in response to the saving action of Christ, the self-surrendering sacrificial victim.

This theme of self-sacrifice as part of the Christian spiritual journey is as old as Christianity itself. And yet it has been problematic for women within the context and history of patriarchal culture. Jesus taught his followers that he came not to be served but to serve, and that they in turn should deny themselves and take up their cross (Mark 8.34). But in patriarchal societies where women are subordinate to men, traditional doctrines of sacrifice and self-denial have been interpreted from a masculine point of view. In a society where men dominate in the hierarchical structure, self-denial for men does not entail relinquishing power over women; while self-denial for women usually entails serving male privilege.

The notion of self-sacrifice – surrendering oneself to serve others' needs in imitation of Christ – has resulted in women being offered damaging feminine aspirations that are either impoverished or unrealistic, based as they are on obedience, passivity and non-assertiveness. Mary Wollstonecraft insightfully argued in the late eighteenth century against this sort of subservient feminine ideal:

> Connected with man as daughters, wives, and mothers, [women's] moral character may be estimated by their manner of fulfilling those simple duties; but in the end, the grand end of their exertions should be to unfold their own faculties and acquire the dignity of conscious virtue.   (1996:14)

Wollstonecraft illustrates the historical tendency within patriarchal culture to inculcate a life of dependency in women where service to men and family defines the boundaries of respectability and virtue. She foreshadows succeeding thinkers who have investigated this inculturated tendency among women towards a sort of self-denial and non-assertiveness, usually for the sake of men. It is a form of abnegation that constrains women's attainment of full personhood and creativity. Classical theology has historically valued selfless love: indeed, Scripture affirms and upholds this virtue. The problem arises when selfless love, and other virtues, are interpreted and expounded solely through the male lens. When this happens, as Wollstonecroft points out,

> man, from the remotest antiquity, found it convenient to exert his strength to subjugate his companion, and his invention to shew that she ought to have her neck bent under the yoke, because the whole of creation was only created for his convenience and pleasure.
>
> (1996:14–15)

Taught to embrace the feminine ideal promoted by male-dominated culture, women have suppressed their own desires and will, a self-destructive impulse which has often resulted in their failure to develop their full potential. They may be so concerned with the needs of others or so dependent on others' authority or approval that they lack a sense of personal autonomy or integrity.

The Church has promoted the notion of sacrificial self-giving as a virtuous aspiration, without taking account of gendered differences in the nature of such self-giving. It has encouraged women to suppress their desires and impulses and to restrict themselves to the maternal or domestic role. Patriarchal culture, in its interpretation of self-sacrifice, has assumed that the male way of thinking is that of all of humankind, male and female. This kind of correlation impoverishes theology, in part because of the way it discourages women from taking responsibility for their own self-actualization. In such an environment, sharing, serving and self-giving figure above independence and self-actualization in women's cultural aspirations. The Church has continually failed to challenge women to full adult freedom, with the result that many women have been unable to achieve selfhood and responsible agency, necessary attributes of Christian maturity.

Women's compulsion to self-sacrifice has a long history, in the Church and in wider society. In the Middle Ages, for example,

church teaching emphasized the value of physical suffering in potentially leading to redemption, and an individual's suffering could be
offered in prayer as a form of service. At the same time there was an
expansion in religious institutions and movements which offered
increasing opportunities for women to express their piety, and this
they often did through a variety of ascetic practices. Since the feminine was associated with nature and matter and therefore particularly prone to evils of the flesh, pious women were drawn to fasting
as a form of self-mortification that expiated evils associated with
corporeality. Some female mystics, notably Catherine of Siena,
adopted extreme froms of fasting and sleep deprivation as part of
their austere regime. In Catherine's case, self-starvation may have
contributed to her early death.

Feminist thinkers have criticized the traditional notion of personal salvation through self-denial and self-sacrifice. They argue that
it is oppressive to many women who are already suffering from low
self-worth and lack of identity induced by a male-dominated culture
in which the feminine is non-normative and nontheomorphic – that
is, not in the image of God. Fran Porter, for instance, conducted a
study of the status of women in the Church today. She found that
when women are subordinate to men and where care and nurture
are associated with the feminine, then 'self-denial itself finds a gendered expression within Christianity' (2004:61). Hence, for women,
the combination of Christian self-sacrifice and self-denial within a
dualistic framework diminishes women's struggle towards full personhood; women sacrifice themselves for the sake of men. Porter
finds this to be the case in her interviews with a range of women; for
some there is a growing sense of self-worth, but for other women
she notes 'a sense of unworthiness, of failure, guilt, and of being
nothing special' (2004:62).

Valerie Saiving addresses the question of self-sacrifice in her
seminal article 'The Human Situation: A Feminine View' ([1960]
1979). Saiving bases her argument on the central fact of sexual difference and early divergence between masculine and feminine sexual
development. She maintains that many characteristic themes in the
way theology explores the human condition – for instance anxiety,
estrangement, self-assertiveness, will-to-power, exploitation, objectification of other – are androcentric in nature and do not address
the needs of contemporary women. 'The temptations of woman

as woman', she maintains, 'are not the same as the temptations of man *as man*' (1979:37). Temptations born out of the basic feminist character structure cannot be described in terms of pride and will-to-power, but are better suggested, according to Saiving, by 'triviality, distractibility and diffuseness; lack of an organising center or focus; dependence on others for one's own self-definition . . . in short, underdevelopment or negation of the self' (1979:37).

The propensity towards self-effacement and dependence upon others for identity can lead to self-abnegation whereby a woman may fail to develop her God-given gifts which in fact would enrich her service to God and to others. An emphasis on self-sacrifice, for instance, can lead victimized women to blame themselves for violence that has been perpetrated on them. Women thus take the blame for not being more self-giving and loving. Una Kroll, priest and writer, offers a concrete example of a victim spirituality when she records that in her youth, it was fashionable for Christian women to be victims – that is, to be 'expected to immolate themselves in service, either through the sacrificial life of a holy nun or through giving themselves wholly to the service of their husbands and children' (2001:120). Women who have been taught to aspire to the sacrificial ideal, often closely associated with the icon of the devoted mother, constantly disregard their own needs for those of others, whether husband, children, parents or work colleagues, while at the same time they feel guilty for not giving more or are torn between their own needs and others' demands.

The traditional emphasis given by the Church to the role of wife, mother and carer has reinforced discriminatory practices against women in public, social, religious and business spheres. The *Report on Women and Religion* for the Council Of Europe, written from a political perspective, notes that religious stereotyping reinforces women's and men's traditional positions in society and denies them the opportunity to take on responsibilities traditionally shouldered by the other sex. The result is that women are not encouraged to take up responsibilities outside the home. In Catholic and Orthodox dominated areas in particular, 'the labour participation rates of women and the number of women in parliament are amongst the lowest (Spain being a notable exception)' (Zapfl-Helbling, 2005:7).

This report confirms the fact that even in the developed world, a woman's identity still rests mainly in her role as carer of others.

This is a model which can be used to excuse the subordination of women's identity, so that they are coerced, for instance, into forgiving and forgetting men's violent or sexually abusive behaviour towards them. I am aware, for example, of a clergy wife who suffered physical and mental violence at home, but whose situation was never brought into the open (either by her or by others) because of her husband's public role as parish priest.

The notion of self-sacrifice is intimately linked with that of the theological concept of *kenōsis*, denoting self-emptying. Christians, aspiring to the likeness of Christ, seek to empty themselves of their own will in order to be receptive to God's perfect will. The question of whether the model of *kenōsis* is a helpful one for women has, since Saiving's article, been extensively debated by feminist writers. Some argue that the theme of self-emptying and self-abnegation is unhelpful as a paradigm for women. Sarah Coakley, however, offers a defence of some form of *kenōsis* as compatible with Christian feminism, embracing 'spiritual paradoxes of "losing one's life in order to save it"' ([1990] 1996:83). For Coakley, silent prayer offers a medium that enables vulnerability and personal empowerment to be held together by 'creating the "space" in which non-coercive divine power manifests itself' (1996:84) – crucial for Coakley in her understanding of Christian feminism. This is not the sort of vulnerability that invites abuse or self-repression, but a means of 'personal empowerment, prophetic resistance, courage in the face of oppression, and the destruction of false idolatry' leading to the birthing of new self (1996:110–11).

Finding ourselves through self-offering to and communion with God is an ancient wisdom which Coakley has reworked through the lens of Christian feminism. While inappropriate self-sacrifice can be self-defeating, there can also be a constructive form of self-sacrifice, an expression of outward-looking love that maintains in balance the nurture of self and care for others. This is surely a positive and encouraging theme within a culture where women have struggled to find selfhood. It goes some way to providing a mode of being that retains a sense of self that women are beginning to achieve, while also allowing that self to find abandonment in a God who can be trusted to gift us with the personal becoming that was always our promise.

Following Saiving, feminist theology has sought to re-examine traditional categories of sin and redemption in the light of research into sexual difference. Daphne Hampson, for example, argues that salvation in the Protestant theological tradition is seen as the breaking of self-centredness, of the sinful ego, to form a new self. She questions whether this analysis is appropriate for women, who have generally not suffered from an egotistical self, or experienced domination of others. 'Rather than breaking the self', she comments, 'women . . . need to come to themselves' (1996b:127). She suggests that a better way for women to envisage salvation is as a healing of the self, 'as a person coming to be all that she may be in a network of relationships' (1996b:127).

The problem in a nutshell is that men are characteristically burdened with a sin of pride that stems from too great a sense of the self, while women's abiding sin is one of sloth – not when it comes to serving others but in developing their own potential. And this is only now being addressed. At last, we can be free of the idea that self-affirmation for women is inconsistent with the feminine. Even in the realm of that most conservative institution, organized religion, we are finally moving away from the feminine norm of self-sacrifice in the form of self-denying, subservient roles that engender a sense of guilt and neurosis. Women can flourish only with the final withering of the notion that their passive self-abnegation is a just punishment for the sin of being a woman.

Entering into society entails entering into the symbolic. Women, then, must find their own language so that they can become full subjects of culture. Many women may choose to express this language in the traditionally 'feminine' form of the care and nurture of others. But the liberated woman takes on this role as a free agent rather than as an object of cultural assumptions and pressure to conform to a stereotypical ideal. Self-sacrifice thus becomes active rather than reactive – and perhaps also innovative, subversive and countercultural. I recently came across an extraordinary example of such a person when I travelled around Central America. Rigoberta Menchú is a Guatemalan peasant woman who as a child suffered terrible ordeals and injustices when her parents tried to stand up for the rights of native Indian peoples. She drew on her religious commitment, her training as a catechist and her feminist ideas to pursue her political revolt, which she continued even after losing close members of her family in horrendous circumstances. Her commitment to the cause led her to abstain from marriage and motherhood, crucial roles for women in her culture, in order to further her work in establishing political and social justice. She was awarded the Nobel Peace Prize for her work in 1992. (Her recollections are recorded in Burgos-Debray, 1984).

I have looked at some of the problems caused by deep-rooted fears about women's generative powers and taboos associated with the menses, and how these have affected the lives of women. What, then, is the symbolic effect of the advent of the woman who is a priest? What is the impact of the collision that occurs with the female priest, where the person called to represent Christ at the altar is simultaneously the object of ancient fears about the polluting and potentially evil charge of the menstruant? Can we reinterpret this historically pernicious symbolic association in a way that enriches the Christian narrative and is healing for all women and men? These are the questions I consider in the next chapter.

7

New covenant, new confidence –
the woman priest

'Drink this, all of you; this is my blood of the New Covenant'

When I and three other women were priested in a church in the city of Bath, the bishop announced at the service of ordination that this was an historic occasion for the diocese of Bath and Wells since it was the first time in its history that a bishop had priested what he called 'an all-female cast'. What he did not mention to the congregation was that we would not be observing the ancient tradition of prostrating ourselves before the laying-on of hands, something I have noted and found very moving in other ordination services I have attended. One very practical reason for our omitting this ritual was that one of our number was due to give birth within a matter of weeks.

I have shown in previous chapters that the priest who is a woman carries a great range of symbols associated with the feminine that apparently collide with those symbols traditionally associated with spirituality, with the numinous and with the divine. For some this collision causes anxiety and discomfort; for others it is liberating and enriching. I shall now look at whether and how the woman priest reconciles, challenges and revisions ancient symbolic associations connected with purity, blood and sacrifice.

Women and sacrifice in the Anglican tradition

The decision to ordain women – and therefore necessarily to admit to priesthood people who menstruate, who get pregnant and who give birth – was symbolically a highly charged event for the Church. That women priests include those who are of childbearing age is significant in that the symbolism evoked by them is freighted with that fear and loathing associated, as we have seen, with women's bloodshed through menstruation and childbirth. Frances Drake, priest for ten years, reports that following her ordination several male clergy would no longer speak to her or shake hands with her: 'It would appear that I had become unclean to them overnight' (Drake, 2004:15). She was once hissed at in the sanctuary during a service of the Eucharist and told not to touch the altar, or it would have to be re-consecrated (2004:16). Grace Elliott, one of the first few women superintendents of the Church of the Lord, an African indigenous church in Ikorodu Agbowa, Epe, records that there remains some contention about women being ordained: 'Now women do the same as men. However, there is still controversy on women presiding at Baptism and Holy Communion, and whether women should be allowed to enter the altar while they are menstruating' (Elliott, 2000:2).

The symbolism of blood is not only ingrained deeply in the texts of Christianity and other religions; it is also deeply subversive, especially in relation to the feminine. Women's blood has, in male-dominated religions, kept them away from the practice of sacrifice. When I was visiting an ancient Mayan temple site in Mexico, I asked the local guide (himself of Mayan descent) whether there had been female shamans, and whether they took part in human sacrifice. He answered that there had been some female shamans in early Mayan culture, but that these had disappeared after the practice of human sacrifice had been introduced. His explanation for this was that women did not need to partake in such sacrifice because they gave blood in the course of childbirth. I found an interesting comparison here with my own religious tradition. According to my guide, a woman's childbearing capacity made it unnecessary for her to partake in human sacrifice. In Judaeo-Christian history, this capacity rendered her ritually impure and therefore unable to perform sacrifice. In either case, the result was that sacrifice was an all-male domain.

The question arises as to what it is about the theology of sacrifice that is incompatible with womanhood (and arguably so inimical to women's interests) while at the same time dominating liturgical practice and shaping the identity of the Church. The issue of the woman priest in relation to blood sacrifice is problematic, not least at a psychological level; but it is also subversive in the sense of de-stabilizing the dominant male-centred religious symbolic order and in revealing powerful feminine symbols that promote women's self-actualization. The exclusion of women from the practice of sacrifice is addressed by Luce Irigaray who, as we have seen, accords a central focus to the body as the locus of divine revelation. She attributes humanity's alienation from divinity and nature to a patriarchal order where redemption is effected through denial of the body and through sacrifice performed by men (1993:75–88). Irigaray credits the objectification of women by men in Western male-dominated culture to the child's Oedipal sacrifice of its desire for the maternal body, the act of 'original matricide' on which Western religious thought, society and culture operate (1993:11). The result of this logic is a culture of hostility towards women and nature, both of which are closely associated with the body of the mother. The feminine is always described in terms of deficiency or atrophy, as the other side of the sex (the male) that alone holds a monopoly on value.

How, then, can women initiate certain rites that allow them to live and become women in all dimensions? Irigaray argues that lack of regard to sexual difference, leading to the objectification of women and their exclusion from the social order, lies at the heart of every discourse. Hence, as I noted earlier, her project is to suggest a way of thinking that is not centred on the masculine – something we can only imagine, since it has yet to be realized. As part of this project, she seeks to expose those blind spots of theology that currently conceal the feminine as a locus for the divine. This lack of acknowledgement for the feminine is a particularly problematic issue with regard to women and sacrifice. Investigations in the field of sociology, anthropology and psychology reveal sacrifice to be an almost universally male practice aimed specifically at excluding, controlling and diminishing the powers of women. Women's blood – evidence of the fecundity, mystery and power of women themselves – carries a heavy positive and negative charge which patriarchal society always strives to keep in check. The menstrual woman is associated with mysterious forces for both good and evil, beyond the control of men, resonating with unpredictability and chaos. The male imagination links female physiology with impurity and potential pollution, signalling otherness.

Man comes to know who he is by discovering that he is not woman. As a developing child he is drawn to the maternal body but in his struggle to develop identity and autonomy he sees that he must transcend the vulnerabilities of remaining dependent on the mother figure. Woman is other, and otherness begets the need for the exercise of control by those in power in religion and in society. Man's identity is preserved through avoidance of the pollution of the other, often by the imposition of a taboo. The boundary between the feminine and the masculine must be established and patrolled, with a clear recognition of what is pure and what is impure.

One such boundary, according to Irigaray, is the Eucharist from which (in her Roman Catholic tradition) women are excluded from celebrating. Here, she argues, men have banished women from the sphere of the divine while relying on women's resources. When the priest recites the Eucharistic Prayer, Irigaray wonders whether, 'according to the rite that celebrates the sharing of food and that has been ours for centuries', he should be reminded that 'he would not be there if our body and our blood had not given him life, love, spirit. And that he is also serving us up, we women-mothers, on his communion plate.' Women cannot celebrate the Eucharist, she continues, since 'If they were to do so, something of the truth that is hidden in the communion rite would be brutally unmasked' (1993:21). Part of that truth, according to Irigaray, is the Church's manifest misogyny in allowing women's bodiliness to be posited as the focus of sin and in modelling itself on a father-son genealogy where women are ignored or reduced to the status of mother. Christianity, in the context of masculine society, has celebrated sacrifice at the expense of woman.

Maintaining patrilineal descent

The male-centred logic of sacrifice in Christianity and in other religions has been examined from a sociological point of view by Nancy Jay. Noting its universally male exclusivity, she comments: 'In no other major religious institution is gender dichotomy more consistently important, across unrelated traditions, than it is in sacrifice' (1992:xxiii). She observes, in the gender-related social logic of the ritual, the polarity of social meaning between sacrificial purity and the pollution of childbirth, and asks what it is about childbirth that can be undone only by sacrifice (1992:284). If women ever perform sacrificial rituals, it is as virgins or crones, not childbearers. Jay notes the symbolic opposition between sacrifice and childbirth in Israelite culture, where sacrifice removes or brings to an end the pollution effected by childbirth or menstruation. She contends that the practice of sacrifice, in maintaining patrilineal descent through fathers and sons, transcends dependence on childbearing women. It identifies not biological but social and religious descent, confirming membership of the group. In Christianity, the lineage is the Apostolic succession of clergy, with a line of descent whereby authority is passed from father to father, through the one Son. By this means – through father and son and never mother and daughter – is obtained integration into the 'eternal' social order transcending mortality. Sacrifice expiates the consequences of having been born of woman and integrates the eternal patrilineage, allowing the patrilineal group to transcend both mortality and birth. Sacrifice overcomes the hiatus in the line of descent from father to son caused by the need to rely on women who are outside the patrilineal line to bear children. Hence, in Jay's words, 'sacrifice is doubly a remedy for having been born of woman' (1992:40).

Disagreement between the Anglican and Roman Catholic Churches over ordination of women has in some quarters centred on the sacrificial nature of the Eucharist. For the (Catholic) Sacred Congregation for the Doctrine of the Faith, the ordination of women is an insuperable obstacle to reconciliation between the two denominations, including a consensus on the nature of sacrifice. Sacrifice is seen by some to identify and maintain an exclusively male line of descent that was broken in the Church of England in the sixteenth century. From a sociological point of view, the Eucharist can be seen in terms of recognizing the power of sacrifice as a ritual instrument for upholding lasting male-dominated social order. Bearing in mind the religious import of blood and sacrifice, we can see why women are less accepted as priests where the symbolic significance of sacrifice in worship, and the concomitant role of the priest, are analogically highly developed.

Jay's argument that sacrifice is a means of maintaining lines of patrilineal descent has been utilized by William Beers in his book *Women and Sacrifice*. He draws on anthropology and developmental psychology to examine male violence in blood sacrifice and its implications in religion and culture, including ritual and social structures, driven by male narcissistic anxiety, that control and subordinate women. Beers contends that the meaning and origin of blood sacrifice lie not just in the patrilineal superstructure of a society, but also in the closely correlated psychological structure. This he examines, concluding that his work suggests a disquieting view of male psychology and religion and, building on Jay's sociological work, that 'men seek to control lineal descent out of their own male psychological structure' (1992:11–12). In his view, blood sacrifice is a deeply evocative ritual practice which affects us so viscerally that 'intellectual rationalization – the so-called logic of sacrifice – never fully satisfies' (1992:10). He applies the insights of self-psychology, a major movement in psychoanalysis and psychotherapy in the United States, to examine gender specificity in sacrifice, tracing it to the differentiated early development of women and men. Two terms used in self-psychology and of relevance here are self-object and narcissism. A self-object experience is one (usually with other people) that nurtures the self and defines the experience of self and self-esteem. Narcissism refers to the weak, vulnerable self attempting to uphold self-cohesion and reinforce self-esteem.

Beers notes the male violence inherent in blood sacrifice: 'Like others I too have been lured by the darker existential question of what motivates men to do what they do. Why do they make things bleed and die in the name of the sacred?' (1992:10). He relates the violence of blood sacrifice to other forms of male violence, including the subordination of women, which he associates with the psychological function of sacrificial ritual. The desire for children and for immortality are part of a male psychological constellation involving the envy, desire and fear of women. The patrilineal kinship system is based on a binary opposition of a father/mother, male/female dichotomy. Males feel more threatened by factors affecting their sense of self-esteem, prestige and power because they have experienced the omnipotent maternal self-object as Other, rather than experiencing themselves (as females do) as subjective extensions of the self-object. Men can never identify fully with that self-object as women can. They also feel more anxious than women about marginality, which threatens their more rigid ego boundaries and induces narcissistic anxiety, 'the psychological place where men and women most differ with regards to marginality' (1992:139).

Women identify more easily with and internalize marginality, whereas men respond with a narcissistic experience of dread. The ambivalent anxiety of men about women is articulated in symbolic ritual blood sacrifice. The male psychological apparatus experiences sacred pollution as a threat of self-disintegration, which can lead to rage and possibly violence. Beers explains that this is what happens in expiation sacrifice. When the male senses the threat of fragmentation from the self-object, he feels disgust. That which evokes disgust he classifies as 'not-me', and he symbolically embodies this in a surrogate or substitute victim which he kills or scapegoats. The self-object is (psychologically) split into good and bad parts; and for men, these split-off parts are usually experienced around women, sex and childbirth.

The ritual violence of sacrifice is, according to Beers, an ancient means by which men identify with each other as men, gaining self-affirmation and self-validation, while separating themselves from women. This conceals the male desire for identifying with and gaining power over the maternal self-object. Hence, ritual blood sacrifice embodies male and male-identified anxiety and men's symbolic attempts to grasp and control the experienced power of women. We can see this in the early Church with patriarchy's efforts to maintain the male descent group through the apostolic succession by means of the eucharistic re-enactment of Christ's sacrifice. These efforts quickly culminated in the establishment of a patrilineal, sacerdotal priesthood and the exclusion of women from the ecclesiastical hierarchy.

For Beers, the ritual consumption of Christ's body parallels that of the nurturing body of the mother. This substitution of male for female is a logical outcome of a theology of sin reflecting 'the male psychological experience of an intrusive maternal self-object (i.e. defilement) and separation from the same self-object (i.e. abandonment)' (1992:176–7). The fraction of the bread, representing the sacrifice of Christ, symbolizes 'the fragmentation of the self resulting from the intrusive idealized maternal self-object' (1992:177). The sacrifice becomes the definitive self-fragmentation, which negates the power of the defiling and abandoning maternal self-object, replacing it with a nurturing, masculine holy communion, undefiled and un-abandoned.

An ingrained fear and resentment of the power of women still linger, especially around the practice of ritual sacrifice. Indeed, according to Beers, despite the fact of women's ordination to the priesthood, the 'male function of sacrifice psychologically precludes women from performing the act' (1992:167).

Gender, sacrifice and the woman priest

Where does this discourse about gender and sacrifice leave women, and particularly women priests, in relation to the Eucharist? The evident deep-rooted association of death and gender in Western culture links women with nature, corporeality, impurity and sin while suppressing the significance of the maternal body and of birthing and nurturing. The body of the mother induces both longing and desire, anxiety and fear, leading to strategies of control and suppression. If blood sacrifice, with its connotations of death and violence, is a male-centred remedy for having been born of woman, whose function is to control and diminish women, then is it possible for the woman priest to preside with integrity at the eucharistic rite? Can she assume that she is able to perform sacrifice with psychological validity or, as Beers argues, is this an impossibility? Is sacrifice solely the prerogative of men, an act so intimately associated with the male psyche and with male-dominated society that women neither have a place in it, nor should desire to, since it perpetuates the male remedy for having been born of woman and upholds the patriarchal social structure?

Feminists claim that theology begins in experience. If women's experience in relation to sacrifice is one of perceived impurity and hence exclusion and diminishment of selfhood, then does this not for women call into question the validity of the concept and practice of sacrifice itself? By presiding at the Eucharist, are women simply acting as honorary men in a rite that for men remedies maternal birth?

The issue of the woman priest and sacrifice appears to present a cultural and psychological impasse. I suggest, however, that a solution lies in developing the concept of natality proposed by Grace Jantzen. I have already noted Jantzen's project to reverse the preoccupation with death inherent in masculinist structures of thought by taking account of ourselves as natals as much as mortals. Her idea of natality, rooted in the maternal, the bodily and the material, seeks to uncover new possibilities based on the acknowledgement of birth and hence of the embodied and gendered, the physical and material.

She does not address the issue of Eucharist or sacrifice directly. However, I am taking her emphasis on natality, and so on birth and nurturing, and her proposal for a theology of flourishing, as a starting point to explore alternative interpretations of sacrifice more appropriate to feminine thought and experience. In other words, I am looking for a way of understanding sacrifice that can counterbalance traditional symbols linked to death with symbols linked to birth and nurturing, and so help to overcome the difficulty of sacrifice as at heart an exclusively male prerogative. Jantzen's proposal of a concept of natality disrupts the ancient connection of the male with spirit and goodness and the female with nature and sinfulness. Traditional interpretations of Christ's death, involving punishment and expiation, can be balanced in a theology of flourishing with Jesus as a model for what it means to become divine.

An implicit concept of natality and its outworking in Christian worship is evident among a number of contemporary feminist writers. Irigaray promotes alternative methods of resolving conflict that do not imitate the sacrificial violence that is the territory of men (1991:146). She looks to the rhythms of nature and cycles of fertility as an alternative source for women's rites, arguing that women's fertility, their bodies and blood, need to be symbolized. For her, the solution to the 'murder of the mother', exemplified in exclusively male sacrifice, is to assert the genealogy of women in order for women to enter fully into culture. She envisions a humanity cleansing itself of the sin of sexual indifference by means of a woman celebrating the Eucharist with her mother, 'giving her a share of the fruits of the earth blessed by them both'. Thus she might be 'hallowed by her identity as a woman' (1993:21).

Jay's sociological work has been used in feminist studies in the psychology of religion to reflect on the role of the woman priest in sacrifice (see, for instance, Raab, 1997; Ross, 1993). From a psychological point of view, it has been argued that female priests, in sacrificing, are performing a radically transformative function. There is a very powerful female symbolism evoked by the sacrificing woman priest, which is as yet not clearly defined. When women sacrifice, they subvert the old symbol system that has long excluded the maternal. The woman at the altar symbolizes, among other things, the worshipper's experience of God as mother, and hence notions of nurture, connection and sensuality. These are all pre-Oedipal themes which, through symbolic association, become more evident in the Eucharist when women are celebrants. Women's priesthood, then, rehabilitates to language and culture the maternal body hitherto sacrificed by patriarchal religion.

The symbolism of fertility and fecundity associated primarily with the feminine and with the concept of flourishing is in fact already present in the Eucharist. There is the reminder of rebirth in Christ, of the shedding of blood in order to bring life, and of the call to feed and to nurture. How appropriate, then, for the priest who symbolically mediates that maternal symbolism, that nurturing with the body and blood of Christ, to be a woman. She challenges, revivifies and enriches ancient Christian symbols, so that, for instance, birth, a potent signifier, can be seen along with death as a type of sacrificial giving. Una Kroll observes that when she presides at the Eucharist, she is aware of the close analogy between the bloody death of Christ – his suffering to bring in the New Covenant – and childbirth, where 'women hurt and bleed to bring new life into the world' (2001:118). This potent symbolism resonated with me on one day in particular, when I celebrated the Eucharist – actually in the same church in which Una had ministered – with the knowledge that my daughter was in full labour with (as I found out just after the service) her first daughter. As I elevated the host, the birthing analogy became intensely present to me, along with the wealth of images associated with the maternal divine.

These experiences are testimony to the powerful symbolism of the Eucharist in relation to female generative power. There may well be other ways in which the female celebrant, in enriching the ancient symbolism of the Eucharist and its historic association with male separation, will subtly change sacramental theology and practice. Sociological and psychological research has highlighted women's empathy with the other, their sense of interconnectedness and reluctance to make separations. The woman celebrant heightens the symbolism of the Eucharist not as a strictly male, hierarchical ritual but as a meal to be prepared and shared and offered in hospitality. Hence our understanding of the sacramental becomes broader and deeper where the multifaceted symbolism is carried by both male and female celebrants.

Traditional interpretations of the Eucharist, as we have seen, have been inclined to uphold patriarchal authority (including that of

the male clerical elite) on the one hand, while denying and excluding women's experience and power on the other. But the renewed and
revitalized understanding symbolized in the female celebrant provides
a useful counterbalance. It reconnects the sacrament with daily, embodied life, and acknowledges the corporeal and the sensual – in other
words, it is grounded in a thoroughly incarnational theology. It is a
basis for a positive theology of sacrifice from a feminist perspective,
because it confirms that the divine is indeed disclosed through the
medium of the feminine as well as that of the masculine.

Women's priesthood encourages this opening up of the symbolism of sacrifice to incorporate the nuances of sexual difference. By
this means we no longer have to think of sacrifice solely in terms
of death and violence. Nor do we have to sit uncomfortably with the
explanation of sacrifice as a male practice performed as a remedy
for maternal birth. The female celebrant allows us to balance these
interpretations with those of feminine qualities of birthing and nurturing, of gift and flourishing, that reflect the maternal divine.

The practical outworkings of such a shift in the traditional symbolism associated with an all-male sacrificial system are articulated
by Linda Walter, a minister of the chalice in Australia:

> I stand in the sanctuary with a brimming chalice of red fragrant
> wine in my hands . . . I know how to put this cup to these lips. I am
> mother. I stoop and rise. I am nurse. I am woman who knows about
> blood . . . No one has to show me how to do this. I have been doing
> it all my life it seems. I am at home in the sanctuary in this supremely
> ordinary act – this sacrament which focuses all our acts of feeding,
> all our meals, all our ordinary day to day relating and depending on
> one another.   (2003:15)

Walter's remarks resonate with maternal symbolism – the shedding
of blood in order to bring forth new life. And this symbolism is more
appropriate to women's experience and imagination than that of
violence and death. In short, they accord with the notion of natality, which allows women priests (and all women) to bring their own
way of knowing to the eucharistic rite and so to celebrate with
validity and integrity. When the Church recognizes these aspects of
sacrifice, then women will not simply have to bend under the yoke
of its traditionally male-dominated culture and practices – or give
up the struggle and leave, as many have. Instead, the Church will not

only acknowledge these differences but welcome and exploit them, since they bring yet greater richness to the panoply of religious symbolism that informs doctrine and practice. The subversive nature of women's presence in the priesthood is perhaps nowhere more evident than at the altar, where the entire culture of the exclusively male practice of blood sacrifice is now challenged and reinterpreted by a new iconoclastic symbolism grounded in the feminine.

Feminine symbolism may have its subversive core in the issue of blood, but it extends to all aspects of religious (and other) experience. Until the advent of the woman priest, such symbolism was hardly visible in the Anglican tradition (except in those high church communities where the Virgin Mary plays a significant part in devotional life). The past generation or so of women looked for identity with few appropriate models of the feminine, religious or otherwise, except for the ancient dual figures of the virgin and the whore. Generations of girls have been taught that to be a 'good' woman – that is, a respectable wife and mother or a celibate spinster – equates with the repression of sexuality, of sensuality, of enjoyment of bodiliness. A woman's learnt sense of herself is thus put out of kilter when trying to reconcile her self-worth as a virtuous person and any image of herself as a sexual, passionate creature.

There has been a chronic dearth of feminine archetypes that could give meaning and direction to women's desires and aspirations. With regard to sexuality and sensuality, popular role models through the twentieth century remained hardly more nuanced and complex that those of Mary Poppins (respectable, asexual and buttoned up) and Madame Butterfly (tragic, lonely courtesan). Since the 1990s, with its 'girlpower' zeitgeist and the emergence of 'ladette' culture, we have seen the phenomenon of young women pursuing a more overtly sexual idea of femininity, one that often mimics attitudes and behaviours traditionally associated more with young men. But this has happened in a way which, many feminists would argue, renders them as little more than eroticized objects of the male gaze, conforming to male desire, rather than autonomous, liberated women.

In this milieu of very mixed messages about the feminine, the woman priest – with all the attendant symbolism of sexual difference and of the maternal divine – provides an archetype that encourages women in their quest for selfhood. Ever greater numbers of women are now entering the Anglican priesthood. We may, then, be seeing the beginning of a far-reaching development that not only acknowledges women's presence and experience but also celebrates the powerful charge and symbolism inherent in the feminine which is mediated by women, not least in their blood, and which validly reflects aspects of the maternal divine.

In the last chapter I looked at the notion of self-sacrifice, and suggested that we may finally be putting to rest the assumption that, for women, self-sacrifice necessarily takes the unhealthy and non-redemptive form of self-denial and subservience. A woman today should be able to enter into self-sacrifice as the chosen option of a free and responsible agent. The woman priest provides a model of this valid and responsible form of self-sacrifice. The nature of priestly vocation is shaped around obedience, humility and spiritual poverty, borne of *kenōsis* in the imitation of Christ. The priestly role necessarily involves a degree of self-sacrifice in the form of special training, personal discipline and self-giving service to others. At the same time, priesthood carries a level of public authority, traditionally the usual domain of men and exercised in leadership, in worship, in preaching and so on. A woman's calling to the priesthood has required her to enter into an overwhelmingly male clerical caste, an alien culture at times hostile to her presence. And, in order to fulfil her vocation, she has been called to take up that authority which is still very novel for women in the long history of the Church, and still not wholly accepted, even by her own fellow male ministers. Hers is an example of self-sacrifice that, at least until the last decade, has been innovative and countercultural, and which continues to subvert the male-dominated culture of the clerical establishment.

A model for our time

The notion of radically free, possibly subversive human agency is, I suggest, a key theme for a theology of women's priesthood. Using Jantzen's concepts of natality and flourishing, we can counterbalance the traditional symbolism of death and violence around the rite of sacrifice with the symbolism of maternal care and nurturing of new life, of embodiment, of gift and fecundity, of sexuality and the nuances of sexual difference. The female priest evokes a greater

abundance of possibilities in our religious imagination as it acknowledges and incorporates the feminine and subtly changes the psychic
dynamics of our relation to the divine.

The notion of *kenōsis*, as I argued in the last chapter, has traditionally been interpreted in a way that has scapegoated women and
left them subject to victimization. This disempowering interpretation can be addressed by a theology of self-sacrifice that encourages,
not passive suffering for its own sake, but a conscious abandonment
in God, engendering a birthing of the self through personal empowerment that overcomes previous assumptions justifying low
self-esteem. The practising woman priest, while always conscious
of her unworthiness before God to represent Christ and his Church,
has necessarily gone through a protracted period of spiritual formation, of selection and of training. She therefore witnesses to others
that women are not inevitably constrained by a tendency to the sin
of sloth that causes a failure to develop the self.

Since she is herself in a representative position, she renders outdated the tendency to correlate maleness with all human experience and encourages responsibility, in women especially, to strive for
self-actualization in the image of God. Her own being as a woman
encourages other women to realize their ultimate goodness and
value – a pattern of being which many women do not adopt easily.
By the nature of her calling, she witnesses to the efficacy of constructive self-sacrifice that seeks to serve others in the edification of
the Church, including the development of personal spiritual gifts.
In having found herself through being birthed into a new life in
Christ, she serves as a model to other women to develop a relationship with God that encourages them to find their own language in
the process of their personal becoming. The countercultural effect of
such a process is to destabilize those unbalanced gendered symbols
that propagate or reinforce unjust patterns of inequality.

Among other anachronistic notions of inequality that the woman
priest challenges is the notion of ritual impurity associated with
women's blood. Standing at the altar, she finally renders unjustifi-
able the fear and disgust that women's bloodshed evokes. The icon
for sin pictured by Ezekiel as the exposed *niddah*, shunned by society,
is shown to be a product of a male-centred psyche and society which
make an essential correlation between sin and the feminine. She
refutes the assumption that women are essentially nontheomorphic

156

and demonstrates the error of patriarchy in associating the feminine with impurity and inferiority.

The woman priest helps to bring to birth a language of the symbolic and sacramental by which female as well as male sexuality is celebrated as a wholesome part of creation. With her the actual maternal, female body, with its corporality and sensuality, is embraced in the symbolics of the religious imagination. In this way a space is opened up for the acknowledgement and expression of sexual difference in liturgical and sacramental thought and practice. The feminine no longer symbolizes the sinful Eve, the heretic and the harlot depicted by Hosea and Ezekiel. Rather, it is acknowledged as capable of reflecting the divine, and it can now take its full place at the heart of the Christian sacramental tradition, celebrating the central themes of birth and fecundity, sexuality and corporeality that are associated with the maternal body. The fact of women's priesthood bears witness to that capacity of the feminine to signify the divine; and yet there is as yet no fully developed selfhood or language for the feminine. What models are there for women priests, and hence for all women, to aspire to? What images from the Christian tradition can they look to in order to help to develop such a language? I suggest that Mary Magdalene offers such an image.

I noted earlier that the Gospels give a picture of women among Jesus' community playing important and key roles in the climax to the story of his ministry and message. Among these women Mary Magdalene is crucial in spreading the news of the resurrection to the other disciples. Recorded as accompanying Jesus on his travels (Luke 8.2), she is described as one from whom seven demons had come out. Mary is again mentioned by name in the Gospels at several key events leading to the resurrection. In the accounts of Matthew, Mark and John she is among a group of women at the crucifixion, 'looking on from a distance' (Matt. 27.55–56; Mark 15.40–41) or 'near the cross' (John 19.25). Matthew records her presence with another woman while Jesus' body is placed in the tomb (Matt. 27.61).

Mary figures most prominently in the resurrection accounts in all of the Gospels (Matt. 28.1–10; Mark 16.1–11; Luke 24.1–11; John 20.1–8). In the listings of women present, her name usually appears first (even before that of the Virgin Mary), suggesting recognition of her prominent position in the community of followers.

The Lucan resurrection narrative stresses the validity of a woman's testimony as a witness. It is Mary Magdalene and other women who announce the Good News to the men, including the Apostles, whose authority would rest on having witnessed the risen Christ (Luke 24.10), but who at first dismiss the women's words as nonsense. It is left to Peter to overcome the contemporary prejudice against women's testimony and go to look for himself.

John's resurrection account is the most detailed and touching in relation to Mary Magdalene (20.1–18). She starts out one morning to perform the feminine work of anointing Jesus' body, and proceeds to proclaim the Easter message to the men. At the beginning of John 20 the author presents a distraught and grieving woman who, through the next few verses, takes a profoundly significant journey of faith. Initially, Mary (alone in this account) sustains the shock of finding no body in the tomb. In her distressed state, she runs to tell the followers and stands back while Peter and the other disciple investigate the baffling emptiness of the tomb. Once the men have left, she sees two angels, but even God's messengers do not lift her horizons above the present sorrow of her bereavement. On turning away from the tomb she sees Jesus but does not recognize him until he calls her by name (John 20.16), a deeply poignant moment that speaks of the transformation that occurs in the journey of faith when a believer comes to know herself as she is and is liberated to move outward towards others. She is the model for the journey of faith that leads from confusion and anguish to recognition, maturity and informed action.

In response Mary names Jesus: her 'Rabbouni!' (John 20.16) acknowledges their relationship and her role as follower and disciple. Her immediate reaction of clinging to Jesus suggests that she has yet to progress psychologically and emotionally from her present euphoria. Jesus' instructions not to cling physically to him but to spread the message to his disciples, move her on from preoccupation with his physical presence to a spiritual reality – the ascension and beyond – and the commission of an apostolic task.

Mary's pilgrimage thus takes another direction as she obeys the command and sets out with the news of the risen Lord. She moves in her dependency on Jesus from abject lover and mourner to mature apostle. Jesus, the risen Lord, depends on Mary to take forward the resurrection message and inform and inspire those disciples who are destined to become apostles and leaders of the Church. The garden encounter between Jesus and Mary Magdalene is a profoundly healing experience between Creator and creature, redeemer and believer, male and female, that harks back to the original complementarity and friendship of the first humans in the Garden of Eden, interrelating as God had intended.

Despite the courageous pioneering role Mary Magdalene undertook as 'apostle to the apostles', the Western Church has historically tended to emphasize more her part as repentant sinner. Her role as apostle and preacher was still current in the Middle Ages. Stories were told of her travelling to France (where the abbey church at Vézelay was later dedicated to her and was said to hold her remains), thus continuing her aspostolic role (Haskins, 1993:136). But her image as redeemed whore was also prominent. In the Roman Missal of 1570 she was designated as 'penitent' in the liturgy, and readings for her feast day (22 July) included the story in Luke 7.37–50 of the sinful woman who bathed Jesus' feet with her tears and anointed them. There is a traditional understanding that this woman is a prostitute, sister to Mary and Lazarus, and that she is Mary Magdalene; this, however, is not made explicit in the Scriptures. Nevertheless, she has traditionally been regarded as a well-meaning but sinful woman who was led by Jesus to repent. Her image has since inspired many contributions to art and literature and to social action, especially care of prostitutes. She is often depicted in paintings as the repentant sinner holding a jar of ointment with which to anoint Jesus' body.

Her great popularity through history has tended to focus more on her sexuality than on her witness. She embodied the call to conversion no matter how scarlet the sin. Biblical commentators seemed to be preoccupied with the idea that her healing (Luke 8.2) was from a moral or sexual condition rather than a psychological one, although the New Testament never links demoniacal possession directly with sin. She became associated with lust and temptation, vices generally associated with the feminine, and thus portrayed not so much as the prominent female disciple and friend of Christ but as a penitent whore, the type of contrite femininity. The Church, losing sight of the community of equals founded by Jesus, made her manageable and controllable. Conflating her with other penitent female figures rendered her a composite character who typified womankind according to the androcentric Christian tradition.

I suggest that Mary Magdalene can indeed represent all women disciples, including women priests, but that a valid representation requires a shift in the traditional, androcentric and anti-feminist symbolism of some received wisdom. There has in the past few years been a surge in interest in the figure of Mary, including Dan Brown's popular novel *The Da Vinci Code* (2004) and the subsequent film. Yet the interest here, stemming from her supposed relationship with Jesus, remains largely in her sexuality rather than her apostolic calling. The penitent whore, in the male imagination, is more fascinating than the witness to spiritual truths. Through the male gaze, a woman is gauged by her sexuality rather than her spirituality. Male domination of the symbolic system refuses still to accept and respond to the enormous significance of Mary Magdalene's story, which remains subordinated to the still potent symbol of the repentant prostitute. Yet she is the valiant witness, the courageous apostle who can symbolize Christian discipleship for women today, including those aspiring towards priesthood who, like her, struggle to overcome a history of prejudice against their calling as women to represent the risen Christ.

In the light of the debate in relation to women and self-sacrifice, the figure of Mary Magdalene offers the archetype of a woman who has learned to take herself seriously, who knows that what she has to say is important. She is not overcome by the sloth which leads her to deny or ignore her own gifts and calling. Having (at least in legend) been dominated and abused by men, she finds through her relationship with Christ a way to come to herself as a whole, healed and valuable person who can give herself freely to and flourish in her new vocation. She has found her own identity and language as a radically free human agent. As the first witness to the resurrection and as Apostle to the Apostles, Mary initiates a female genealogy which can now be continued through the ordination of women. The figure of Mary Magdalene offers an embodied model on which the woman priest can ground her vocation and ministry, particularly in terms of achieving selfhood, valid discipleship and constructive self-sacrifice.

Mary Magdalene also offers a model for the female priest in her role as representing the broader believing community. This aspect is brought out by Adeline Fehribach in her comments on the fourth Gospel. She suggests that the author drew on contemporary literature and cultural convention to portray Jesus as the messianic bridegroom who enables disciples to become the children of God. To this end, Mary Magdalene functions in the garden encounter as the symbolic bride who is representative of the wider faith community (1998:145). Fehribach views this as a patriarchal device, where the male God weds the 'female' community, with its ancient associations of the woman/bride with unfaithfulness and defilement. A differently nuanced interpretation might, however, link Mary Magdalene as the symbolic bride with the fecundity of the feminine, which carries with it the theme of the fruitfulness of the entire Christian community through its relationship with Christ.

This image of Mary Magdalene surely offers a symbol of the Church as the Bride of Christ that allows women to have confidence in their own calling to discipleship, despite centuries of teaching that, by virtue of their corporeality, their physical function, they are inferior, excluded and ignored. For instance, in her contribution to *The Call for Women Bishops* (2004), Tina Beattie takes the figure of Mary Magdalene, Apostle to the Apostles, to support the ordination of women to the episcopate in order to fulfil the apostolic mission. Women can now celebrate that the Church is being challenged with a radically new way of looking at the position of women ,in the image of God, and of women's religious experience. Women can now claim: we are at last able to accept ourselves as who we are, as daughters of a God who liberates us, who in our own right, through our particular experience, can legitimately take the news of the resurrection into the community. As women work out their true vocations, shedding the constraints of an androcentric fallacy, new possibilities for personal and communal growth will emerge that will enrich the Church and the wider community. True to the example of Mary Magdalene, obedience to divine calling can lead women to a genuine sense of self and to fulfilment in effective ministry.

To sum up, the woman priest demonstrates that the assumption that women's blood is ritually impure or defiling is finally being challenged and eroded in many cultures today. Representative as she is of an institution which traditionally upheld and promulgated this assumption, she illustrates the invalidity of this anachronistic belief. The Bride of Christ, according to Revelation, is also the Temple in which Christ lives, the City whose gates are never shut; yet nothing shameful or impure will enter (Rev. 21.25–27). The woman priest, in representing the Body of Christ, witnesses to woman's overcoming of the blame of impurity and shame attached to physiological function. She affirms that bodies are a matter for celebration rather than shame. A body that menstruates does not have to be seen as polluting: it can validly be understood as holy. The implications of this for liturgy are significant: if menstruation is linked not with impurity and shame but with creativity and even sacredness, then this will have consequences in the evolution of worship. If worship carries any transformative potential, then the new and revitalized symbols will have a bearing on women's self-regard and on the treatment and status of women. The potency of women's generative power remains, but it will be celebrated in new, creative ways that are empowering for women and enriching for all believers.

8

Joining hands in the dance

I often glance through the index of a book on a shop or library shelf, to check whether it covers the areas that I am interested in reading about. Anyone taking a look at the index in this book before reading it might be surprised at what they see. There are entries here – ministry, prayer, worship, Eucharist – which you would expect to find in any book on the theology of priesthood. But there are other entries which have not usually appeared in previous books on this subject: sex, taboo, impurity, otherness, natality, menses. These are among the words that carry a great deal of symbolic association with women, and which therefore now have a bearing on priests who are women and on the priesthood as a whole. They carry symbolic meanings attached to the feminine which have hardly figured among the holy spaces, objects and practices of patriarchal culture, but which can now be mined, embraced and utilized so that the Church's worship and ministry can flourish.

The woman priest has caused a collision between the community's tradition and the continuing revelation that informs Christian identity. This collision has given rise to new interpretations, embedded in women's experience and spirituality, which have begun to enrich and deepen our narrative of faith, and also to engender changes in that ongoing narrative. The shift she causes in the identity of priesthood necessarily means a shift also in the Christian story which the priest represents. As the symbol and narrative of the liturgy engage with the worshipper, so new interpretations and insights will arc from the 'text' of the liturgy to the life of the believing individual and community.

Two symbolic figures that have repeatedly appeared in these pages are those of the bride and the whore. In the vision described by the author of Revelation, the figure of the Church as the Bride of Christ wears fine linen woven from the 'righteous deeds of the saints' (Rev. 19.8). With respect to a theology of women's priesthood, the work of the saints that is woven into the bride's wedding linen entails the task of achieving full personhood for all people, women and men, through the recognition of sexual difference, so that all can find their true identity in God's image. Women's priesthood rescues the image of the bride from an interpretation grounded exclusively in male-dominated culture. It refutes a bride metaphor based on an assumption of woman as subordinate, less godlike and more prone to sin. The whoredom associated with the redeemed bride no longer rests with the inferiority and impurity attached essentially to the feminine. It must now be attributed to the idolatry of a masculinist religious culture that has feared, suppressed and devalued the feminine. A developing theology of women's priesthood redeems all women, and all excluded people, from voicelessness. This is not a new message: it is woven into the warp and weft of the gospel of redemption that is open to all people without distinction.

I have argued here for sexual difference to be treated as a basic philosophical category: the feminine is different (but not inferior to) the masculine, and carries its own distinct range of symbolic meanings. Women and men have ways of being and thinking that are related to their sex and gender, and no one sex can define all that it is to be human or represent the divine. But how does this theory work out in the lives and experience of real people practising their faith? In my own ministry, both in England and in Wales, where some years have elapsed since the first clergywomen were ordained, I have had time to reflect on how clergy and laypeople respond to a priesthood of both sexes. Many people I meet, both lay and ordained, readily acknowledge that female priests bring a welcome and different range of skills and experience to pastoral ministry. But this, vitally important as it is, has not been my first concern here. Rather, I have been asking about any difference in the symbolic meanings associated with a priesthood of both sexes. However, these meanings pre-figure the relationship between priest and people, people and God. So they influence strongly the way that members of the church family understand themselves and act in the world. And of course pastoral issues arise from these ways of understanding and acting.

There are those for whom the gender of the priest is of no consequence. A retired clergyman told me that he discerns no significant difference when a woman presides at the Eucharist, but that it feels perfectly normal and natural. Others, however, have experienced strong and profound reactions. Another colleague told me that, during her training for ordination, about a year elapsed before she attended a Eucharist led by a woman. She then realized that she had missed being ministered to by a female priest. The service spoke to her in a different way in terms of her sense of identity and her relationship with God.

A sense of something missing in a Church with an all-male priesthood has been a source of pain to many. A woman who now attends church regularly spoke to me of the difficulty she had felt in the 1980s in belonging to an institution that, she felt, denied women's equal status, their spiritual maturity and their own religious experiences, It was the eventual ordination of women that caused her to risk re-engagement with the Church. For some, then, the woman priest represents recognition, acceptance and equality for women which they had felt was lacking.

Some people find that a female presence can be healing, symbolizing as it does the journey made by those who have previously felt outside the norm of church or society. The woman priest stands with all outsiders who exist in some form of otherness, an embodied expression of all those whom a male-centred culture has forgotten, ignored or repressed. All these people can now travel forward from rejection to inclusion, from reviled to beloved, from otherness to potential selfhood. The chaplain of a women's prison told me that she felt she offered a model of church for women whose contact with the masculine world has been painful, damaging and alienating. She noted the incarnational symbolism of women meeting together in solidarity at the Eucharist. It became something shared, something done together, in a way that was different from when a male chaplain presided. For her, it showed that there is 'a way to God through the feminine, that as women they too are part of creation and therefore of incarnation'.

The pain felt by women in a man's world was mentioned also by a Roman Catholic woman who attended a service I was leading. She told me afterwards that it was the second time she had witnessed a women presiding, and that it seemed very natural to see a woman representing Christ: 'Many women experience men as cruel – and a woman priest helps them appreciate the compassion that is Christ.' For her, that sense of compassion was conveyed partly by the timbre of my voice, something she described as 'most precious – few, if any, men can convey it'. In some churches, the female voice is still not heard from the pulpit, the choir or the altar, and where it is heard, its symbolic weight still causes strong reactions. A colleague told me of her surprise that she has received more comments about her voice than anything else. She remarked that both women and men have been moved by hearing the Eucharistic Prayer spoken by a female: 'Perhaps, for women, hearing the story of salvation spoken by a woman helps them to claim that story for themselves – and maybe for men the timbre of a woman's voice has associations of motherhood and comfort and acceptance.'

The symbolic resonance between the woman priest and motherhood is something which others have commented on. I asked a male colleague about his response to celebrating alongside a female priest. He answered that it made him aware that 'it is not maleness that creates a priest. Like a woman in labour, there is an element of self-giving sacrifice, in order that life may come to exist in others.' As we have seen, there is a range of symbolic associations around the maternal, including those connected with self-giving and serving. I'm aware, through talking with female colleagues, that the business of preparing the altar at the Eucharist and clearing it after the distribution of Holy Communion is very rooted in many women's experience of home and family. A vicar mentioned that she is concerned about making sure the children feel included at the Eucharist: 'We are the ones who have always served meals to families. We're connected with nourishment and feeding. We wouldn't prepare a meal at home without feeding the children.' As it happens this vicar is not a wife or a mother; but nevertheless she is deeply aware of the symbolic meanings associated with her sex. I once led worship in a modern church with a kitchen in an adjoining room. Making use of this opportunity, I put some dough to bake during the service, so that the bread I broke and shared at Holy Communion arrived straight out of the oven. The newly baked, delicious-smelling bread conveyed the symbolism of the Lord's Supper in a particularly vibrant way, and perhaps one that was especially fitting for a minister who is also a woman, a wife and a mother. Revisiting the tradition of Christian symbol and narrative through the figure of the woman priest does not mean rejecting or veering away from orthodox Anglican faith. We can remain faithful to the Christian tradition while also breaking open new or previously overlooked interpretations. We are constantly called to reinterpret, in the light of continuing revelation, our common narrative of faith. Ancient, polysemic symbols that have always been integral to the Christian story have to be heard again so that meanings emerge which are true and appropriate to our time and place, and freed from gendered connotations that ignore or devalue the feminine. As this happens we have to adjust our understanding of individual and communal identity and consider the principles by which we live. Hence we revise our response to ethical issues as new insights are gained.

The recognition of sexual difference leads to the consideration of difference in many areas of life. In the Church, we are now seeing the working out of the principle of unity in difference and diversity in matters of gender, sexuality, culture, physical ability and many other fields. For instance, the female priest challenges purely mas-culinist assumptions about women's sexuality as it is portrayed and understood both in contemporary society and in Scripture. As sexual difference is acknowledged and acted upon, then both women and men are given the opportunity to attain full personhood as creatures of God and as equal subjects of culture. The woman priest has a major role to play in this cultural transformation. As a repre-sentative both of the divine and of the Body of Christ, she carries in her bodily presence a symbol of the triune God who is neither male nor female but in whom both women and men have their being. She models for all women their capability to be channels for speak-ing about and reflecting the divine in a way which is different from that of the male.

A woman priest who is aware of the symbolic resonance she bears is enabled to develop her ministry in a way that is distinctive and appropriate to her calling and to her gender. She will be con-fident to preach and to lead worship with authority from her own gendered perspective, not because she is acting as an honorary man but because she carries that authority *as a woman*. She will interpret the text of Scripture and liturgy in a way that may challenge well-established traditions, but which is nevertheless part of that ancient tradition of discerning divine revelation for our own time and place. She will lead worship in a way that recognizes and honours the fem-inine, and so draws in many who have previously found a deafening absence of the female voice in worship. Old traditions will be woven in with new words and rituals that carry meaning for the many who have remained invisible – the survivor of sexual abuse, the couple who have suffered a miscarriage, the girl who has reached puberty, the woman who has reached menopause.

A woman priest who is affirmed and valued in her ministry can confidently challenge the social construct of male hegemony that has prevailed in our narrative of faith. In making available a symbolic space for the feminine in our religious imagination, she opens the way for women to develop their full potential through and not despite their experience of church. She foreshadows the days when every woman will affirm that she is no longer on the margins but is able to become what God intends her to be, because she knows that she is truly a human person created in the image of God.

One consequence of the theology I am proposing would be to see women and men living and working together, as members of the Body of Christ, in mutually supportive respect, encouragement and collaboration. Within some parts of the Anglican Communion, the clergy now have the opportunity to minister together as equal partners. For the first time they are able together to create a sacred space that embraces gendered difference, that celebrates sexed identity and that upholds the integrity of the feminine. This is something of great value to many women and men. A male priest remarked to me that, on the day that the first women were priested in Wales, he felt that the Church's ministry was finally being made whole, and that 'something that was missing in a purely male domain had now come into the equation'. With male and female now represented at the altar, he sensed that we are now able to grasp 'a fuller understanding of the nature of God'. An American priest told me that he first observed a woman and a man concelebrating in Washington DC. 'It was a moving experience that brought me to more fully appreciate the paradox that God embodies the masculine and feminine, yet transcends the division between male and female'. In short, as another colleague remarked, 'Together we are representing God between us'.

Where both men and women preside at the Eucharist, then they together offer worshippers multiple and polysemic images of the divine and of creation. These enriched images are destabilizing entrenched, male-dominated symbols that have become solidified and resistant to new interpretations. The effect is to loosen the limitations of traditional religious language where its meaning is no longer always fully adequate or appropriate. The way we talk about divine gender, for example, is never straightforward, and as we have seen in Chapter 3, it is open to a variety of configurations. A fluid interplay of familiar and newly retrieved meanings enlarges and enhances our lexicon of religious language. But to fully realize the potential of the new range of symbols made available by the female priest, she must be able to exercise her ministry as a woman with a sense of self and a way of being that are her own and are not borrowed from masculinist discourse. She must be set free from any language or practice that discriminates against her sex, whether in terms of outright rejection of her ministry or in terms of subtle, even unconscious, discrimination within groups where male attitudes and behaviours have traditionally been normative.

Efforts in gaining full acceptance of women in the Church are currently focused in England and Wales on the episcopacy and the prospect of women bishops. The Christian tenet that God is neither male nor female is embodied in liturgy and ministry where both female and male priests celebrate the Eucharist and minister together. Yet this tenet cannot be fully symbolized or expressed until women are represented in all the ministries of the Church, including that of the episcopate. While women are still denied this ministry, then the Church will rightly be seen to remain a bastion of male domination, tightly controlled by a male clerical elite.

An episcopate open to women will doubtless cause the sort of collision that we have seen in other public spheres, where there is a mismatch between what is expected of a woman and what is expected of a person with high status and authority. The Church, like other public institutions, will be seen to challenge the still prevailing view that women are essentially more suited to lower status roles in the public sphere – assistant teachers rather than heads, 'soft' portfolios in government, pastoral ministry in the Church. An episcopate of both sexes is likely to promote the flourishing of other clergywomen in their vocations. While the question of women bishops was recently debated (and rejected) in the Church in Wales, Canon Mary Stallard remarked that women clergy she met in New York, where women bishops are accepted, seemed to be numerous, empowered and hopeful about the future. She wondered whether the presence of female bishops helps other American women to be 'more confident in exploring their vocation and in offering themselves in service in the diversity of Christian ordained ministries'

(Bayley, 2006:6). An American colleague told me how important the presence of women's leadership was to the younger generation of girls. He served for several years in the diocese of Washington with Bishop Jane Holmes Dixon. When the bishop finally retired, his young daughter asked him, 'Can men be bishops?'

In Britain, we still await the ministry of a female bishop. Listening to other women clergy telling of their struggle and pain (and aware of my own story), it is clear to me that, without an episcopate that embodies sexual difference, women who are called to ordination will continue to run the risk of being incorporated into excluding and even abusive hierarchical systems of domination. And all women in the Church will continue to be subject to age-old beliefs and practices that associate the feminine with low status and inferiority.

Clergywomen need now to engage with debate about their full acceptance; and such a debate must necessarily explore the possibilities of radical structural change to an historically male-dominated institution. The model of work and leadership that might be offered by women bishops could be invaluable in supporting other women clergy working within structures and theologies developed to serve male-defined interests. Church institutions still function according to masculinist principles that can be ignorant of and inimical to women's interests. The more women are restricted in developing their ministry and participating in leadership, the more they will feel conflicted, demoralized and exhausted. An environment that does not truly accept one's full humanity, authority or equality is a hard and inhospitable place of ministry.

My aim is not to replace a male hegemony with a female one. I am in no way trying to privilege women's experience or ways of knowing. I have no desire to valorize the feminine over and against the masculine. This would simply reproduce the dualistic polarity that characterizes patriarchy. What I am arguing for is harmonious, fruitful and mutually respectful partnership between the sexes. This image of a God-given male–female bond is one that the Church, represented by male and female priests celebrating together, can effectively symbolize, both in the Eucharist and in day-to-day ministry.

In January 2007 I attended a Eucharist at Llandaff Cathedral to mark the tenth anniversary of the ordination of women priests in Wales. The celebrant was Bishop Christina Odenberg of the Lund

Figure 2 Right Reverend Christina Odenberg, Bishop of the Lund Diocese, Sweden and the then Bishop of Bangor, Wales, the Right Reverend Tony Crockett.

Diocese, Sweden. At the close of the service, as a band played 'We Are Marching in the Light of God', Bishop Christina joined hands with the then Bishop of Bangor, Bishop Tony Crockett, and they danced together up the central aisle. I think that the image of those two bishops, moving in mutual esteem and harmony, sums up much of what I have been arguing here in developing a theology of women's priesthood.

Bibliography

Allott, Kenneth, ed. (1962), *The Penguin Book of Contemporary Verse*, London, Penguin.

Anderson, Pamela Sue and Beverley Clack, eds (2004), *Feminist Philosophy of Religion*, London, Routledge.

Angier, Natalie (1999), *Woman: An Intimate Geography*, London, Virago.

Ashby, Geoffrey (1988), *Sacrifice: Its Nature and Purpose*, London, SCM Press.

Augustine, Saint (1961), *Confessions*, trans. R. S. Pine-Coffin, Harmondsworth, Penguin.

Balmforth, Henry (1963), *Christian Priesthood*, London, SPCK.

Banks, Robert (1994), *Paul's Idea of Community*, Peabody, MA, Hendrickson.

Barr, Liz and Andrew (2001), *Jobs for the Boys? Women Who Became Priests*, London, Hodder & Stoughton.

Barth, Karl (1958), *Church Dogmatics* vol. 3 part 1, trans. J. W. Edwards, O. Bussey and Harold Knight, Edinburgh, T&T Clark.

Barth, Karl (1960), *Church Dogmatics* vol. 3 part 2, trans. Harold Knight, G. W. Bromily, J. K. S. Reid and R. H. Fuller, Edinburgh, T&T Clark.

Beattie, Tina (1999), *God's Mother, Eve's Advocate*, CCSRG Monograph Series 3, Bristol, University of Bristol.

Beattie, Tina (2003), *Woman*, London, Continuum.

Beattie, Tina (2004), 'A Roman Catholic's View on the Apostolicity of Women', in Harris and Shaw, eds, *The Call for Women Bishops*, pp. 69–82.

Beattie, Tina (2006), *New Catholic Feminism: Theology and Theory*, London and New York, Routledge.

Beers, William (1992), *Women and Sacrifice: Male Narcissism and the Psychology of Religion*, Detroit, Wayne State University Press.

Belenky, Mary Field, Blythe McVicker Clinchy, Nancy Rule Goldberger, Jill Mattuck Tarule (1986), *Women's Ways of Knowing: The Development of Self, Voice and Mind*, New York, Basic Books.

Berger, Teresa (1999), *Women's Ways of Worship: Gender Analysis and Liturgical History*, Collegeville, MN, The Liturgical Press.

Boff, Leonardo OFM (1979), *The Maternal Face of God: The Feminine and Its Religious Expressions*, New York, Harper & Row.

Bouyer, Louis (1968), *Eucharist*, Notre Dame, IN, University of Notre Dame Press.

Bradley, Harriet (1995), *Fractured Identities: Changing Patterns of Inequality*, Cambridge, Polity Press.

Bradley, Ian (1995), *The Power of Sacrifice*, London, Darton, Longman and Todd.

Brenner, Athalya, ed. ([1993] 1997), *A Feminist Companion to Genesis*, Sheffield, Sheffield Academic Press.

Brenner, Athalya, ed. (1995), *A Feminist Companion to the Latter Prophets*, Sheffield, Sheffield Academic Press.

Brink, André (2000), *On the Contrary*, London, Vintage.

Burgos-Debray, Elisabeth, ed. (1984), *I, Rigoberta Menchú, An Indian Woman In Guatemala*, trans. Ann Wright, London, Verso.

Bynum, Caroline Walker (1982), *Jesus as Mother: Studies in the Spirituality of the High Middle Ages*, London, University of California Press.

Bynum, Caroline Walker (1987), *Holy Feast and Holy Fast: The Religious Significance of Food to Medieval Women*, London, University of California Press.

Bynum, Caroline Walker, Stevan Harrell and Paula Richman, eds (1986), *Gender and Religion: On the Complexity of Symbols*, Boston, Beacon Press.

Cameron, Deborah (1992), *Feminism and Linguistic Theory*, Basingstoke, Palgrave.

Cameron, Deborah (2007), *The Myth of Mars and Venus: Do Men and Women Really Speak Different Languages?* Oxford, Oxford University Press.

Chopp, Rebecca (1991), *The Power to Speak: Feminism, Language, God*, Eugene, OR, Wipf and Stock.

Chopp, Rebecca S. and Sheila Greeve Davaney, eds (1997), *Horizons in Feminist Theology: Identity, Tradition, and Norms*, Minneapolis, Augsburg Fortress.

Christ, Carol P. and Judith Plaskow, eds (1979), *Womanspirit Rising: A Feminist Reader in Religion*, New York, HarperSanFrancisco.

Clark, Elizabeth A. (1983), *Women in the Early Church*, Wilmington, DE, Michael Glazier Inc.

Clark, Peter (1984), 'Snakes and Ladders: Reflections on Hierarchy and the Fall', in Furlong, ed., *Feminine in the Church*, pp. 178–94.

Coakley, Sarah (1996), 'Kenosis and Subversion: On the Repression of "Vulnerability" in Christian Feminist Writing', in Hampson, ed., *Swallowing a Fishbone?*, pp. 82–111.

Coakley, Sarah (2002), *Powers and Submissions: Spirituality, Philosophy and Gender*, Oxford, Blackwell.

Countryman, L. William (1998), *Dirt, Greed and Sex*, Philadelphia, Fortress Press.

Crockett, William R. (1989), *Eucharist: Symbol of Transformation*, New York, Pueblo Publishing.

D'Costa, Gavin (2000), *Sexing the Trinity: Gender, Culture and the Divine*, London, SCM Press.

Davies, Jon and Gerard Loughlin (1997), *Sex These Days: Essays in Theology, Sexuality and Society*, Sheffield, Sheffield Academic Press.

De Boer, Esther (1997), *Mary Magdalene: Beyond the Myth*, trans. John Bowden, London, SCM Press.

De Mello, Anthony (1990), *Awareness*, London, Fount Paperbacks.

De Troyer, Kirstin, Judith A. Herbert, Judith Ann Johnson, Anne-Marie Korte, eds (2003), *Wholly Woman, Holy Blood: A Feminist Critique of Purity and Impurity*, Harrisburg, PA, Trinity Press International.

Dierks, Sheila Durkin (1997), *WomenEucharist*, Boulder, CO, WovenWord Press.

Dix, Dom Gregory ([1945] 1982), *The Shape of the Liturgy*, Westminster, Dacre Press.

Donghi, Antonio (1997), *Actions and Words: Symbolic Language and the Liturgy*, trans. W. McDonagh and D. Serra, Collegeville, MN, The Liturgical Press.

Douglas, Mary (1966), *Purity and Danger*, London, Routledge.

Drake, Frances (2004), Untitled essay in Gould, ed., *God's Work of Art*, pp. 13–17.

Elwes, Teresa, ed. (1992), *Women's Voices: Essays in Contemporary Feminist Theology*, London, Marshall Pickering.

Exum, J. Cheryl (1996), *Plotted, Shot and Painted: Cultural Representation of Biblical Women*, Sheffield, Sheffield Academic Press.

Farley, Margaret (1990), 'Feminist Theology and Bioethics' in Loades, ed. *Feminist Theology*.

Fehribach, Adeline (1998), *The Women in the Life of the Bridegroom*, Collegeville, MN, The Liturgical Press.

Fiorenza, Elisabeth Schüssler (1983), *In Memory of Her: A Feminist Theological Reconstruction of Christian Origins*, London, SCM Press.

Fiorenza, Elisabeth Schüssler (1998), *Sharing Her Word: Feminist Biblical Interpretation in Context*, Edinburgh, T&T Clark.

Fox, Kate (2004), *Watching the English: The Hidden Rules of English Behaviour*, London, Hodder.

Frayn, Michael (1999), *Headlong*, London, Faber and Faber.

Furlong, Monica (1991), *A Dangerous Delight: Women and Power in the Church*, London, SPCK.

Furlong, Monica, ed. (1984), *Feminine in the Church*, London, SPCK.

Furlong, Monica, ed. (1988), *Mirror to the Church: Reflections on Sexism*, London, SPCK.

Galloway, Kathy (1995), *Getting Personal: Sermons and Meditations*, London, SPCK.

Gilligan, Carol (1982), *In a Different Voice: Psychological Theory and Women's Development*, London, Harvard University Press.

Gjerding, Iben and Katherine Kinnamon, eds (1983), *No Longer Strangers: A Resource for Women and Worship*, Geneva, WCC Publications.

Glover, David and Cora Kaplan (2000), *Genders*, London, Routledge.

Golden, Stephanie (1998), *Slaying the Mermaid: Women and the Culture of Sacrifice*, New York, Harmony Books.

Gould, Graham, ed. (2004), *God's Work of Art: Essays Celebrating the Tenth Anniversary of the Ordination of Women to the Priesthood in the Church of England*, London, Women and the Church.

Green, Alison (2007), 'The Priest, the Body, the Bride and the Whore: Towards a Theology of Women's Priesthood', unpublished doctorial dissertation, Roehampton University.

Greenberg, Blu (2003), 'In Defense of the Daughters of Israel', in Soskice and Lipton, eds, *Feminism and Theology*, pp. 229–43.

Greenwood, Robin (1994), *Transforming Priesthood: A New Theology of Mission and Ministry*, London, SPCK.

Grenz, Stanley (2001), *The Social God and the Relational Self: A Trinitarian Theology on the Imago Dei*, London, Westminster John Knox Press.

Grey, Mary (1989), *Redeeming the Dream: Feminism, Redemption and Christian Tradition*, London, SPCK.

Grey, Mary (2001), *Introducing Feminist Images of God*, Sheffield, Sheffield Academic Press.

Gunton, Colin (2003), *Father, Son and Holy Spirit: Towards a Fully Trinitarian Theology*, London, T&T Clark.

Halkes, Catharina J. M. ([1989] 1991), *New Creation*, trans. C. Romanik, London, SPCK.

Hall, Kira and Mary Bucholtz, eds (1995), *Gender Articulated: Language and the Socially Constructed Self*, London, Routledge.

Hampson, Daphne ([1990] 1996), *Theology and Feminism*, Oxford, Blackwell.

Hampson, Daphne, ed. (1996a), *Swallowing a Fishbone?* London, SPCK.

Harris, Harriet and Jane Shaw (2004), *The Call for Women Bishops*, London, SPCK.

Haskins, Susan (1993), *Mary Magdalene: The Essential History*, London, Pimlico.

Hebblethwaite, Margaret (1984), *Motherhood and God*, London, Geoffrey Chapman.

Henry, Matthew (1721), *An Exposition of the New Testament Vol. VIII*, London, William Mackenzie.

Hines, Mary E. (1993), 'Community for Liberation' in LaCugna, ed., *Freeing Theology*, pp. 161–84.

Hoekema, Anthony A. (1986), *Created in God's Image*, Carlisle, Paternoster Press.

Hopko, Thomas, ed. (1999), *Women and the Priesthood*, Crestwood, NY, St Vladimir's Seminary Press.

Hurcombe, Linda, ed. (1987), *Sex and God: Some Varieties of Women's Religious Experience*, London, Routledge & Kegan Paul.

Irigaray, Luce (1974), *Speculum of the Other Woman*, trans. Gillian C. Gill, New York, Cornell University Press.

Irigaray, Luce (1991), *Marine Lover of Friedrich Nietzsche*, trans. Gillian C. Gill, Chichester, Columbia University Press.

Irigaray, Luce (1993), *Sexes and Genealogies*, trans. Gillian C. Gill, Chichester, Columbia University Press.

Irigaray, Luce, ed. (2004), *Key Writings*, London, Continuum.

Isherwood, Lisa and Dorothea McEwan, eds (1996), *An A to Z of Feminist Theology*, Sheffield, Sheffield Academic Press.

Jamieson, Penny (2004), 'Authority' in Harris and Shaw, *The Call for Women Bishops*.

Jantzen, Grace (1984), *God's World, God's Body*, London, Darton, Longman and Todd.

Jantzen, Grace (1995), *Power, Gender and Christian Mysticism*, Cambridge, Cambridge University Press.

Jantzen, Grace (1998a), *Becoming Divine: Towards a Feminist Philosophy of Religion*, Manchester, Manchester University Press.

Jay, Nancy (1992), *Throughout Your Generations Forever: Sacrifice, Religion and Paternity*, Chicago and London, University of Chicago Press.

Johnson, Elizabeth A. ([1992] 2002), *She Who Is: The Mystery of God in Feminist Theoretical Discourse*, New York, Herder & Herder, Crossroad.

Joseph, Alison, ed. (1990), *Through the Devil's Gateway*, London, SPCK.

Joy, Morny, Kathleen O'Grady and Judith Poxon, eds (2003), *Religion in French Feminist Thought*, London, Routledge.

Keillor, Garrison (1986), *Lake Wobegon Days*, London, Faber and Faber.

Keller, Catherine (1986), *From a Broken Web: Separation, Sexism and Self*, Boston, Beacon Press.

Kimel Jnr, Alvin F., ed. (1992), *Speaking the Christian God: The Holy Trinity and the Challenge of Feminism*, Leominster, Gracewing.

King, Ursula (1989), *Women and Spirituality*, Basingstoke, Macmillan Education.

King, Ursula, ed. (1995), *Religion and Gender*, Oxford, Blackwell.

Kroll, Una (2001), *Anatomy of Survival*, London, Continuum.

LaCugna, Catherine M., ed. (1993), *Freeing Theology: The Essentials of Theology in Feminist Perspective*, San Francisco, HarperSanFrancisco.

LaCugna, Catherine Mowry (1991), *God for Us: The Trinity and Christian Life*, New York, HarperCollins.

Lee, Harper (1960), *To Kill a Mocking Bird*, London, Pan Books.

Leopold, Aldo ([1949] 1970), *A Sand County Almanac*, New York, Ballantine.

Loades, Ann, ed. (1990), *Feminist Theology*, London, SPCK.

Lohfink, Gerhard (1982), *Jesus and Community: The Social Dimensions of Christian Faith*, Philadelphia, Fortress Press.

Maathai, Wangari (2007), *Unbowed: One Woman's Story*, London, Heinemann.

Bibliography

Martos, Joseph and Pierre Hegy, eds (1998), *Equal at the Creation*, Toronto, University of Toronto Press.

McElhinny, Bonnie (1995), 'Challenging Hegemonic Masculinities: Female and Male Police Officers Handling Domestic Violence', in Hall and Bucholtz, eds, *Gender Articulated*.

McEwan, Dorothea, ed. (1991), *Women Experiencing Church: A Documentation of Alienation*, Leominster, Gracewing.

McFague, Sallie (1987), *Models of God*, London, SCM Press.

McFague, Sallie (1993), *The Body of God: An Ecological Theology*, London, SCM Press.

Meeks, Wayne (1983), *The First Urban Christian: The Social World of the Apostle Paul*, London, Yale University Press.

Merchant, Carolyn (1980), *The Death of Nature: Women, Ecology and the Scientific Revolution*, New York, HarperSanFrancisco.

Moi, Toril, ed. (1987), *French Feminist Thought: A Reader*, Oxford, Basil Blackwell.

Mollenkott, Virginia R. (1983), *The Divine Feminine: The Biblical Imagery of God as Female*, New York, Crossroad.

Moltmann, Jürgen (1993), *The Trinity and the Kingdom*, trans. Margaret Kohl, Minneapolis, Fortress Press.

Morley, Janet ([1988, 1992] 1998), *All Desires Known*, London, SPCK.

Moses, John (1992), *The Sacrifice of God*, Norwich, Canterbury Press.

Newsom, Carol A. and Sharon H. Ringe, eds (1992), *Women's Bible Commentary*, Louisville, KY, Westminster John Knox Press.

Northup, Lesley A. (1997), *Ritualizing Women*, Cleveland, OH, The Pilgrim Press.

Northup, Lesley A., ed. (1993), *Women and Religious Ritual*, Washington, DC, Pastoral Press.

Nouwen, Henri (2000), *The Only Necessary Thing: Living a Prayerful Life*, London, Darton Longman and Todd.

O'Faolain, Nuala ([1996] 1999), *Are You Somebody? The Accidental Memoir of a Dublin Woman*, New York, Owl Books.

O'Grady, Kathleen, Ann L. Gilroy and Janette Gray (1998), *Bodies, Lives, Voices: Gender in Theology*, Sheffield, Sheffield Academic Press.

Ortlund, Raymond C. (1996), *Whoredom: God's Unfaithful Wife in Biblical Theology*, Grand Rapids, MI, William B. Eerdmans Publishing Company.

Owen, Wilfred ([1920] 1962), 'Insensibility', in Allott, Kenneth, ed., *The Penguin Book of Contemporary Verse*, London, Penguin.

Parsons, Susan Frank, ed. (2002), *The Cambridge Companion to Feminist Theology*, Cambridge, Cambridge University Press.

Porter, Fran (2004), *It Will Not Be Taken Away from Her: A Feminist Engagement with Women's Christian Experience*, London, Darton, Longman and Todd.

Power, David N. (1984), *Unsearchable Riches: The Symbolic Nature of Liturgy*, New York, Pueblo Publishing Company.

Primavesi, Anne (1991), *From Apocalypse to Genesis: Ecology, Feminism and Christianity*, Tunbridge Wells, Burns & Oates.

Proulx, Annie (2002), *That Old Ace in the Hole*, London, Harper Perennial.

Redfern, Alistair (1999), *Ministry and Priesthood*, London, Darton, Longman and Todd.

Rees, Christina, ed. (2002), *Voices of this Calling: Experiences of the First Generation of Women Priests*, Norwich, Canterbury Press.

Ricoeur, Paul (1967), *The Symbolism of Evil*, trans. Emerson Buchanan, Boston, Beacon Press.

Ricoeur, Paul (1995), *Figuring the Sacred: Religion, Narrative, and Imagination*, Minneapolis, Fortress Press.

Robinson, Gene (2008), *In the Eye of the Storm*, Norwich, Canterbury Press.

Ross, Susan A. (1993), 'God's Embodiment and Women' in LaCugna, ed., *Freeing Theology*, pp. 185–209.

Ross, Susan A. (1998), *Extravagant Affections: A Feminist Sacramental Theology*, New York, Continuum.

Royden, A. Maude (1924), *The Church and Woman*, London, James Clarke.

Ruether, Rosemary R. (1985a), *Women-Church: Theology and Practice of Feminist Liturgical Communities*, San Francisco, Harper & Row.

Ruether, Rosemary R. (1985b), *Womanguides: Readings Towards a Feminist Theology*, Boston, Beacon Press.

Ruether, Rosemary R. (1992), *Gaia and God*, London, SCM Press.

Russell, Letty M. (1993), *Church in the Round: Feminist Interpretation of the Church*, Louisville, KY, Westminster John Knox Press.

Russell, Letty M., ed. (1985), *Feminist Interpretation of the Bible*, Philadelphia, The Westminster Press.

St Hilda Community, The St (1991), *The New Women Included: A Book of Services and Prayers*, London, SPCK.

Saiving, Valerie ([1960] 1979), 'The Human Situation: A Feminine View' in Christ and Plaskow, eds, *Womanspirit Rising*, pp. 25–42. First published in *Journal for Religion*, April 1960.

Schaef, Anne Wilson (1992), *Women's Reality: An Emerging Female System in a White Male Society*, New York, HarperSanFransisco.

Schwobel, Christopher and Colin E. Gunton (1991), *Person, Divine and Human*, Edinburgh, T&T Clark.

Senn, Frank C. (1997), *Christian Liturgy: Catholic and Evangelical*, Minneapolis, Fortress Press.

Sherwood, Yvonne (1996), *The Prostitute and the Prophet: Hosea's Marriage in Literary-Theoretical Perspective*, Sheffield, Sheffield Academic Press.

Shiva, Vandana (1989), *Staying Alive: Women, Ecology and Development*, London, Zed Books.

Shorter, Edward (1982), *A History of Women's Bodies*, Plymouth, Basic Books.

Shriver, Lionel (2003), *We Need to Talk About Kevin*, New York, Perennial.

Shuttle, Penelope and Peter Redgrove (1999), *The Wise Wound*, London, Marion Boyars.

Soskice, Janet M. and Diana Lipton, eds (2003), *Feminism and Theology*, Oxford, Oxford University Press.

Stevenson, Kenneth (2002), *Do This: The Shape and Meaning of the Eucharist*, Norwich, Canterbury Press.

Stevenson, Kenneth and Bryan Spinks, eds (1991), *The Identity of Anglican Worship*, London, Mowbray.

Stewart Van Leeuwwen, Mary, ed. (1993), *After Eden: Facing the Challenge of Gender Reconciliation*, Grand Rapids, MI, William B. Eerdmans Publishing Company.

Strachan, Elspeth and Gordon (1985), *Freeing the Feminine*, Dunbar, Labarum Publications.

Tertullian (1869), *On Female Dress*, Book 1, 1 in *The Writings of Tertullian* vol. 1, trans. Peter Holmes, ANCL 11, Edinburgh, T&T Clark.

Thorne, Helen (2000), *Journey into Priesthood: An In-Depth Study of the First Women Priests in the Church Of England*, Bristol, Centre for Comparative Studies in Religion and Gender, Department of Theology and Religious Studies, University of Bristol.

Tong, Rosemarie (1989), *Feminist Thought: A Comprehensive Introduction*, San Francisco, Westview Press.

Trible, Phyllis (1992), *God and the Rhetoric of Sexuality*, London, SCM Press.

Ulanov, Ann Belford (1981), *Receiving Woman: Studies in the Psychology and Theology of the Feminine*, Philadelphia, Westminster Press.

Wakeman, Hilary, ed. (1996), *Women Priests: The First Years*, London, Darton, Longman and Todd.

Walter, Linda (2003), 'A Canterbury Tale', in Soskice and Lipton, eds, *Feminism and Theology*, pp. 13–15.

Ward, Hannah, Jennifer Wild and Janet Morley (1995), *Celebrating Women*, London, SPCK.

Watson, Natalie K. (2003), *Feminist Theology*, Cambridge, William B. Eerdmans Publishing Groups.

Wegner, Judith R. (1988), *Chattel or Person? The Status of Women in the Mishnah*, Oxford, Oxford University Press.

Wiesner, Merry (1990), 'Luther and Women: The Death of Two Marys', in Loades, ed., *Feminist Theology*, p. 123.

Williams, Rowan (1984), 'Women and the Ministry: A Case for Theological Seriousness', in Furlong, ed., *Feminine in the Church*, pp. 11–27.

Wilson, E. O. (1992), *The Diversity of Life*, Harmondsworth, Penguin Books.

Wilson-Kastner, Patricia (1983), *Faith, Feminism and the Christ*, Philadelphia, Fortress Press.

Witherington III, Bill (1990), *Women and the Genesis of Christianity*, Cambridge, Cambridge University Press.

Witherington III, Bill (1998), *Women in the Earliest Churches*, Cambridge, Cambridge University Press.

Wollstonecraft, Mary ([1792] 1996, abridged), *The Rights of Woman*, London, Orion.

Wootton, Janet H. (2000), *Introducing a Practical Feminist Theology of Worship*, Sheffield, Sheffield Academic Press.

Wren, Brian (1989), *What Language Shall I Borrow? God-Talk in Worship: A Male Response to Feminist Theology*, London, SCM Press.

Xinran (2003), *The Good Women of China*, trans. Esther Tyldesley, London, Vintage.

Young, Frances M. (1975), *Sacrifice and the Death of Christ*, London, SPCK.

Zappone, Katherine (1991), *The Hope for Wholeness: A Spirituality for Feminists*, Mystic, CT, Twenty-Third Publications.

Ziesler, J. A. (1983), *Pauline Christianity*, Oxford, Oxford University Press.

Zizioulas, John D. (1985), *Being As Communion: Studies in Personhood and the Church*, Crestwood, NY, St Vladimir's Seminary Press.

Journals

Cornell, Jean (2003), 'Kairos Comes Too Soon: Are Women Priests in Retreat in the Church Of England?', *Feminist Theology* 12.1, pp. 43–51.

Eaton, Heather (2001), 'At the Intersection of Ecofeminism and Religion: Directions for Consideration', *Ecotheology* 6.1, 6.2, pp. 75–91.

Gudorf, Christine E. (1987), 'The Power to Create: Sacraments and Men's Need to Birth', *Horizons* 14.2, pp. 296–309.

Keith Hamnett (2008), 'Why Change the Sense of Hymns?', *Church Times* issue 7574 (May).

Jackson, G. (1998), 'Jesus as First-century Feminist: Christian Anti-Judaism?', *Feminist Theology* 19 (September), p. 85.

Jantzen, Grace (1996), 'What's the Difference? Knowledge and Gender in (Post) Modern Philosophy of Religion', *Religious Studies* 32.4 (December), pp. 431–48.

Jantzen, Grace (1998b), 'Necrophilia and Natality: What Does It Mean to Be Religious?', *Scottish Journal of Religious Studies* 19.1 (Spring), pp. 101–22.

Jonte-Pace, Diane (1997), 'New Directions in the Feminist Psychology of Religion', *Journal of Feminist Studies in Religion* 13.1, pp. 61–9.

Klassen, Ryan (2004), '"As the Image": A Functional Understanding of the *Imago Dei*', *Quodlibet Journal* 6.3 <http://www.Quodlibet.net>.

Kugler, Robert (1997), 'Holiness, Purity, the Body and Society', *Journal for the Study of the Old Testament* 76, pp. 3–27.

Leadbetter, Barry (2004), 'Irene Manton: A Biography (1904–1988)', *The Linnean* special issue 5.

Martin, Alison (2003), 'Luce Irigaray and the Culture of Difference', *Theology, Culture & Society* 20.3, pp. 1–12.

Middleton, J. Richard (1994), 'The Liberating Image? Interpreting the Imago Dei in Context', *Christian Scholars Review* 24.1, pp. 8–25.

Need, Stephen W. (2002), 'Jesus the Bread of God: The Eucharist as Metaphor in John 6', *Theology* 105.825 (May/June), pp. 194–200.

Raab, Kelley A. (1997), 'Nancy Jay and a Feminist Psychology of Sacrifice', *Journal of Feminist Studies in Religion* 13.1, pp. 75–89.

Sawyer, John (1989), 'Daughter of Zion and Servant of the Lord in Isaiah: A Comparison', *Journal for the Study of the Old Testament* 44, pp. 89–107.

Sen, Amartya (1990), 'More than One Hundred Million Women Are Missing', *New York Review of Books*, 37.20 <http://ucatlas.ucs.edu/gender/Sen100M.html>.

Smith, Christine (1993), 'Sin and Evil in Feminist Thought', *Theology Today* 50.2, pp. 208–19.

Soskice, Janet M. (1994), 'Trinity and "The Feminine Other"', *New Blackfriars* (January), pp. 2–17.

Steinberg, Jonah (1997), 'From a "Pot of Filth" to a "Hedge of Roses (and Back)"', *Journal of Feminist Studies in Religion* 13.2 (Fall), pp. 5–26.

Papers, documents, statements

Archbishop of Canterbury's Commission on Urban Priority Areas (1985), *Faith in the City*, London, Church House Publishing.

Archbishops' Council (2006), *Responding to Domestic Abuse: Guidelines for Those with Pastoral Responsibility*, London, Church House Publishing.

Bayley, Raymond, ed. (2006), *Theology Wales: The Ordination of Women to the Episcopate*, Cardiff, Church in Wales Publications.

Blyth, Myra (2001), 'Gender and Diakonia: Go-Betweens and Agents of Change' in Raiser and Robra, eds, *With Love and with Passion*, pp. 154–9.

Church and Society Commission (May 2006), *Gender Mainstreaming in the Church and Society Commission*, Draft Policy Paper, Conference of European Churches.

Elliott, Grace (February 2000), 'An African Perspective' in Lambkin, Anne and Pauline Main, eds, *Celebrating Women's Ministry*, Newsletter, Women's Co-ordinating Group for Churches Together In England, p. 3.

Eucharistic Presidency: A Theological Statement by the House of Bishops of the General Synod (1997), London, Church House Publishing.

Irigaray, Luce (1986), *Divine Women*, trans. Stephen Muecke, Sydney, Local Consumption Occasional Papers 8.

Lambkin, Anne and Pauline Main, eds (2005), *Celebrating Women's Ministry*, London, Women's Co-ordinating Group for Churches Together in England.

Lewis, Alan E., ed. (1984), *The Motherhood of God: Report of the Woman's Guild/Panel on Doctrine Study Group*, Church of Scotland Report to the General Assembly, Edinburgh, Saint Andrew Press.

Liturgical Commission of the General Synod of the Church of England (1988), *Making Women Visible*, London, Church House Publishing.

Penberthy, Joanna (2006), 'Learn from the Past and Build for the Future: Preparing Women for the Episcopate', in Bayley, ed., *Theology Wales*, pp. 12–19.

Raiser, Elisabeth and Barbara Robra, eds (2001), *With Love and with Passion: Women's Life and Work in the Worldwide Church*, Geneva, WCC Publications.

Roman Catholic International Theological Commission (2004), *Communion and Stewardship: Human Persons Created in the Image of God.*

Soskice, Janet M. (1994), 'Blood and Defilement', paper presented to the Society for the Study of Theology conference, Oxford, April 11–14. Published in the *Journal of the European Society for Cartholic Theology* 2, Tübingen.

Stallard, Mary (2006), 'Women Bishops in the Church in Wales' in Bayley, ed., *Theology Wales.*

Zapfl-Helbling, Rosmarie, rapporteur (2005), *Report on Women and Religion*, Doc. 10670, Council of Europe: Committee on Equal Rights for Women and Men.

Index

Index

Johnson, Elizabeth 37, 39, 40–1
Jonah, Book of 53
Judaeo-Christian: creation story 90; culture 65; history 121, 144; scripture 32; tradition 21, 34
Judges, Book of 12
Judith, Book of 32
Julian of Norwich 37, 55
justice 1, 3, 16, 17, 41, 59, 61, 74 79, 87, 91, 93–4, 99, 102, 105, 110, 123, 142

kenōsis 140
Keillor, Garrison 9
Kroll, Una 7, 98, 103, 139, 152

Lamentations, Book of 33
language: inclusive 12, 37–8, 109; male-dominated 12, 32
Last Supper 68, 70, 116
Leadbetter, Barry 77
leadership 1, 70, 84, 99, 103, 107–9, 155
Lee, Harper 133
Leopold, Aldo 89
Leviticus, Book of 116, 124, 127
Liturgical Commission 36
Lot 59, 121
Luke, Gospel of 72, 116, 127, 159
Luther, Martin 23, 132

Maathai, Wangari 93
McFague, Sallie 37
Maitland, Sara 37
Making Women Visible (Liturgical Commission) 36, 37
Malleus Maleficarum 131
Manton, Irene 77
Mark, Gospel of 38, 126–7, 157
marriage 28–30, 32–4, 36, 42, 71–2, 95, 116, 121, 123, 131, 132, 141
Mary Magdalene 1, 157–61
masculine/male 5
Masemola, Manche 122
maternal: body 15, 129, 134, 145, 150, 152, 157; divine 50, 52–65, 99–100, 152–5;

symbolism 50, 60, 98, 110, 131, 152–3
maternity 51, 95
Matthew, Gospel of 31, 69, 126–7, 157
mediator 51, 97, 117, 123
medieval period 55, 87, 124, 130
Menchú, Rigoberta 141
menopause 58, 99, 125, 168
menses 122, 124, 133, 142 163
mercy 53, 74, 105, 110, 136
metaphor 3, 12, 28–9, 31–4, 37, 39, 41–2, 110, 164
Micah, Book of 74, 87, 94
Michelangelo 22
midwife 51, 54 79, 130
miscarriage 58, 99, 130, 131, 168
misogyny 18, 75, 128–34, 146
mission 30, 37, 80, 84, 91, 103, 119, 126, 161
Moltmann, Jürgen 41
Morley, Janet 37
mortal 17, 125, 150; mortal sin 130; mortality 16, 102, 147
Moses 12, 21, 22, 57, 70, 116
Motherhood and God (Hebblethwaite) 37
mutuality 31, 39, 41–2, 49, 59 63, 67, 80, 83, 102, 107

Naomi 32
narrative of faith 4, 12, 73, 163, 167, 168; *see also* institution narrative
natal 16, 74–5, 98, 102, 150; natality 17, 51, 74–5, 79, 101, 105, 113, 150–1, 153
neophyte 53, 54
New Testament 29, 38, 68, 79 126, 159
Noah 116
Nouwen, Henri 71
nurture 51–5, 58, 60, 97, 98, 110, 112–14, 138, 140, 141, 151–2

Obama, Barack 2–3
O'Faolain, Nuala 77
Old Testament 38, 53, 72, 118, 120; *see also* Hebrew scripture

On the Contrary (Brink) 134
oppression 58, 76, 84, 94, 105, 140
ordination 2, 6–9, 44–6, 49, 67, 84, 92, 103–4, 106–7, 143–4, 147, 149, 160–1, 165, 170
Origen 30, 55
otherness 26, 27, 57–9, 61–2, 105, 135, 145, 163, 164
Owen, Wilfred 120

Passover 69–70
patrilineal descent 31, 147–9
patristic era 30, 40; patristic writers 54
Paul the Apostle 6, 11, 26, 27, 116, 118
Penberthy, Joanna 7, 109
perichoresis 40–2, 63, 84, 106, 110
Peter the Apostle 28, 54, 158
phallocentric imagination 34
Pliny the Elder 126, 130
pornography 34, 59, 65
Porter, Fran 138
power, generative 52, 58, 115, 123, 126, 128, 142, 152; reproductive 133
prayer 9, 19, 20, 32, 37, 52, 58, 60, 70, 138, 140, 163; Prayer A 18, 20
pride 59, 139, 141
prostitute 12, 44, 59 *see also* harlotry, whore
Protestant tradition 9, 141; Protestantism 50, 131
Proulx, Annie 87
Proverbs, Book of 39, 59, 110
Psalm 59, 71
purification 116, 122, 130
purity 116, 122–8

Quaker 132

Rachel 59
rape 58–9, 61, 121, 135
rationality 14, 24–5, 46
reason 23–4, 46, 48, 59
reciprocity 40, 49, 67
redemption 18, 27, 47, 68, 73–6, 91, 94, 96–8, 104–5, 114, 136, 138, 140
Redgrove, Peter 133

185